Science and Religion: A Very Short Introduction

VERY SHORT INTRODUCTIONS are for anyone wanting a stimulating and accessible way in to a new subject. They are written by experts, and have been published in more than 25 languages worldwide.

The series began in 1995, and now represents a wide variety of topics in history, philosophy, religion, science, and the humanities. Over the next few years it will grow to a library of around 200 volumes – a Very Short Introduction to everything from ancient Egypt and Indian philosophy to conceptual art and cosmology.

Very Short Introductions available now:

Available soon:

For more information visit our websites
www.oup.com/uk/vsi
www.oup.com/us

Thomas Dixon

SCIENCE AND RELIGION

A Very Short Introduction

OXFORD
UNIVERSITY PRESS

OXFORD
UNIVERSITY PRESS

Great Clarendon Street, Oxford OX2 6DP

Oxford University Press is a department of the University of Oxford.
It furthers the University's objective of excellence in research, scholarship,
and education by publishing worldwide in

Oxford New York

Auckland Cape Town Dar es Salaam Hong Kong Karachi
Kuala Lumpur Madrid Melbourne Mexico City Nairobi
New Delhi Shanghai Taipei Toronto

With offices in

Argentina Austria Brazil Chile Czech Republic France Greece
Guatemala Hungary Italy Japan Poland Portugal Singapore
South Korea Switzerland Thailand Turkey Ukraine Vietnam

Oxford is a registered trade mark of Oxford University Press
in the UK and in certain other countries

Published in the United States
by Oxford University Press Inc., New York

British Library Cataloguing in Publication Data

Data available

Library of Congress Cataloging in Publication Data

Data available

ISBN 978-0-19-929551-7

1 3 5 7 9 10 8 6 4 2

Typeset by SPI Publisher Services, Pondicherry, India
Printed in Great Britain by
Ashford Colour Press Ltd, Gosport, Hampshire

For Emma Dixon

Contents

Preface

Books about science and religion generally fall into one of two categories: those that want to persuade you of the plausibility of religion and those that want to do the opposite. This *Very Short Introduction* falls into neither category. It aims instead to offer an informative and even-handed account of what is really at stake. The polemical passion the subject often generates is an indication of the intensity with which people identify themselves with their beliefs about nature and God, whether they are religious or not. The origins and functions of those beliefs form the subject of this book.

In recent years the topic of 'science and religion' has become almost synonymous, especially in the United States, with debates about evolution. For this reason, two of the six chapters of this book are devoted to evolutionary subjects. The modern American debate about evolution and 'Intelligent Design' illustrates particularly clearly how stories about conflict or harmony between science and religion can be used in political campaigns – in this case relating to the control of education and the interpretation of the First Amendment to the US Constitution.

Historical notions about famous individuals, especially Galileo Galilei and Charles Darwin; philosophical assumptions about miracles, laws of nature, and scientific knowledge; and discussions of the religious and moral implications of modern science, from quantum mechanics to neuroscience, are regular features of science–religion debates today. All of these are scrutinized here.

It is no part of my aim in this book to persuade people to stop disagreeing with each other about science and religion – far from it. My hope is only that it might help people to disagree with each other in a well-informed way.

Acknowledgements

I was first introduced to this fascinating topic, as an
undergraduate student, by Fraser Watts's lectures on theology and
science at Cambridge University, and by John Hedley Brooke's
classic *Science and Religion: Some Historical Perspectives*
(Cambridge, 1991). Subsequently, as a postgraduate, I was taught
at the Universities of London and Cambridge by distinguished
historians and philosophers of science, including Janet Browne,
Hasok Chang, Rob Iliffe, Peter Lipton, Jim Moore, and Jim
Secord. I am indebted to all of them and to the supportive and
stimulating research environment I encountered in Cambridge
both at the Department for the History and Philosophy of Science
and in the Faculty of Divinity. I am also grateful for the support
of colleagues, in more recent years, in Lancaster and London. I
would particularly like to mention Stephen Pumfrey and Angus
Winchester at Lancaster University, and Geoffrey Cantor for his
help with the organization of a conference there on 'Science and
Religion: Historical and Contemporary Perspectives' in July 2007
to mark John Hedley Brooke's retirement. I learned a great deal
from all the contributors to that conference. Most recently I have
benefited from the guidance and encouragement of my colleagues
at Queen Mary, University of London, especially Virginia Davis,
Colin Jones, Miri Rubin, Yossef Rapoport, Rhodri Hayward,
Joel Isaac, and Tristram Hunt. Emilie Savage-Smith and Salman
Hameed have given me much-appreciated guidance on the subject

of Islam and science. At Oxford University Press, Marsha Filion, Andrea Keegan, and James Thompson helped me through the production process with patience, skill, and enthusiasm. Fiona Orbell acquired the images and necessary permissions with great speed and efficiency, and Alyson Silverwood ensured that the text was copyedited to the highest standard. Special thanks are due to those friends who took the time and trouble to read drafts of the text and offer me advice on how to improve it, namely Emily Butterworth, Noam Friedlander, James Humphreys, Finola Lang, Dan Neidle, Trevor Sather, Léon Turner, and especially Giles Shilson. My greatest debt is to my family. The book is dedicated to my sister Emma, who advised me to become an academic and not a lawyer.

List of illustrations

The publisher and the author apologize for any errors or omissions in the above list. If contacted they will be pleased to rectify these at the earliest opportunity.

Chapter 1
What are science–religion debates really about?

In Rome on 22 June 1633 an elderly man was found guilty by the Catholic Inquisition of rendering himself 'vehemently suspected of heresy, namely, of having held and believed a doctrine which is false and contrary to the divine and Holy Scripture'. The doctrine in question was that 'the sun is the centre of the world and does not move from east to west, that the earth moves and is not the centre of the world, and that one may hold and defend as probable an opinion after it has been declared and defined as contrary to Holy Scripture'. The guilty man was the 70-year-old Florentine philosopher Galileo Galilei, who was sentenced to imprisonment (a punishment that was later commuted to house arrest) and instructed to recite the seven penitential Psalms once a week for the next three years as a 'salutary penance'. That included a weekly recitation of the particularly apt line addressed to God in Psalm 102: 'In the beginning you laid the foundations of the earth, and the heavens are the work of your hands.' Kneeling before the 'Reverend Lord Cardinals, Inquisitors-General', Galileo accepted his sentence, swore complete obedience to the 'Holy Catholic and Apostolic Church', and declared that he cursed and detested the 'errors and heresies' of which he had been suspected – namely belief in a sun-centred cosmos and in the movement of the earth.

It is hardly surprising that this humiliation of the most celebrated scientific thinker of his day by the Catholic Inquisition on the grounds of his beliefs about astronomy and their contradiction of the Bible should have been interpreted by some as evidence of an inevitable conflict between science and religion. The modern encounter between evolutionists and creationists has also seemed to reveal an ongoing antagonism, although this time with science, rather than the church, in the ascendancy. The Victorian agnostic Thomas Huxley expressed this idea vividly in his review of Charles Darwin's *On the Origin of Species* (1859). 'Extinguished theologians,' Huxley wrote, 'lie about the cradle of every science as the strangled snakes beside that of Hercules; and history records that whenever science and orthodoxy have been fairly opposed, the latter has been forced to retire from the lists, bleeding and crushed if not annihilated; scotched, if not slain.' The image of conflict has also been attractive to some religious believers, who use it to portray themselves as members of an embattled but righteous minority struggling heroically to protect their faith against the oppressive and intolerant forces of science and materialism.

Although the idea of warfare between science and religion remains widespread and popular, recent academic writing on the subject has been devoted primarily to undermining the notion of an inevitable conflict. As we shall see, there are good historical reasons for rejecting simple conflict stories. From Galileo's trial in 17th-century Rome to modern American struggles over the latest form of anti-evolutionism, known as 'Intelligent Design', there has been more to the relationship between science and religion than meets the eye, and certainly more than just conflict. Pioneers of early modern science such as Isaac Newton and Robert Boyle saw their work as part of a religious enterprise devoted to understanding God's creation. Galileo too thought that science and religion could exist in mutual harmony. The goal of a constructive and collaborative dialogue between science and religion has been endorsed by many Jews, Christians, and Muslims in the modern world. The idea that scientific and religious views are inevitably in tension is also contradicted by

2

the large numbers of religious scientists who continue to see their research as a complement rather than a challenge to their faith, including the theoretical physicist John Polkinghorne, the former director of the Human Genome Project Francis S. Collins, and the astronomer Owen Gingerich, to name just a few.

Does that mean that conflict needs to be written out of our story altogether? Certainly not. The only thing to avoid is too narrow an idea of the kinds of conflicts one might expect to find between science and religion. The story is not always one of a heroic and open-minded scientist clashing with a reactionary and bigoted church. The bigotry, like the open-mindedness, is shared around on all sides – as are the quest for understanding, the love of truth, the use of rhetoric, and the compromising entanglements with the power of the state. Individuals, ideas, and institutions can and have come into conflict, or been resolved into harmony, in an endless array of different combinations.

The leading historian of science and religion John Hedley Brooke writes that serious historical study has 'revealed so extraordinarily rich and complex a relationship between science and religion in the past that general theses are difficult to sustain. The real lesson turns out to be the complexity.' Some of that historical complexity will be explored in subsequent chapters. There has certainly not been a single and unchanging relationship between two entities called 'science' and 'religion'. There are, nonetheless, some central philosophical and political questions that have frequently recurred in this context: What are the most authoritative sources of knowledge? What is the most fundamental reality? What kind of creatures are human beings? What is the proper relationship between church and state? Who should control education? Can either scripture or nature serve as a reliable ethical guide?

Debates about science and religion are, on the face of it, about the intellectual compatibility or incompatibility of some particular religious belief with some particular aspect of scientific knowledge. Does belief in life after death conflict with the findings of modern brain science? Is belief in the Bible incompatible with believing that humans and chimpanzees evolved from a common ancestor? Does belief in miracles conflict with the strictly law-governed world revealed by the physical sciences? Or can belief in free will and divine action, conversely, be supported and substantiated by the theories of quantum mechanics? One of the answers to the question that is the title of this chapter – What are science–religion debates really about? – is that they are about these issues of intellectual compatibility.

What I especially want to emphasize in this *Very Short Introduction* to the subject, however, is that these contemporary contests of ideas are the visible tips of much larger and deeper-lying structures. My aim throughout this book will be to look historically at how we came to think as we do about science and religion, to explore philosophically what preconceptions about knowledge are involved, and to reflect on the political and ethical questions that often set the unspoken agenda for these intellectual debates. In the rest of this introductory chapter, I indicate the kinds of questions I think we should be asking about science and religion, both as sources of individuals' beliefs and as social and political entities, before also briefly introducing 'science and religion' as an academic field.

Encountering nature

Scientific knowledge is based on observations of the natural world. But observing the natural world is neither as simple nor as solitary an activity as it might sound. Take the moon, for instance. When you look up at the sky on a clear night, what do you see? You see the moon and the stars. But what do you actually observe? There are a lot of small bright lights and then a larger whitish circular object. If you had never learned any science, what would you think this white object was? Is it a flat disc, like a kind of giant aspirin? Or is it a sphere? If the latter, then why do we always see the same side of it? And why does its shape change from a thin crescent to a full disc and back again? Is it an object like the earth? If so, how big is it? And how close? And do people live there? Or is it a smaller night-time equivalent of the sun? Finally, perhaps it is like one of the little bright lights but larger or closer? In any case, how and why does it move across the sky like that? Is something else pushing it? Is it attached to an invisible mechanism of some kind? Is it a supernatural being?

Now, if you are well informed about modern science, you will know that the moon is a large spherical rocky satellite which orbits the earth completely about once a month and which rotates once on its own axis in the same time (which explains why we always see the same side of it). The changing relative positions of the sun, earth, and moon also explain why the moon displays 'phases' – with either the entirety or only a small crescent of the illuminated half of the moon visible at a particular time. You may also know that all physical bodies are attracted to each other by a gravitational force in proportion to the product of their masses and in inverse proportion to the square of the distance between them, and that this helps to explain the regular motions of the moon around the earth and of the earth around the sun. You will probably also know that the bright little lights in the night sky are stars, similar to our sun; that the ones visible to the naked eye are thousands of light years away and those observable through telescopes are millions or even billions of light years away; so that to look up at the night sky is to look into the distant past of our universe. But however much of all this you know, you did not find it out by observation. You were told it. You possibly learned it from your parents or a science teacher or a television programme or an online encyclopaedia. Even professional astronomers will not generally have checked the truth of any of the statements made in this paragraph by their own empirical

5

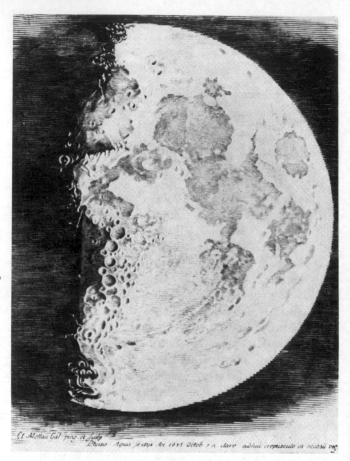

1. The moon as engraved by the artist Claude Mellan from early 17th-century telescopic observations

observations. The reason for this is not that astronomers are lazy or incompetent, but simply that they can rely on the amassed authoritative observations and theoretical reasonings of the scientific community which, over a period of many centuries, have established these facts as fundamental physical truths.

The point is that while it is certainly true that scientific knowledge is based on and tested against observations of the natural world, there is an awful lot more to it than just pointing your sense organs in the right direction. As an individual, even an individual scientist, only the tiniest fraction of what you know is based directly on your own observations. And even then, those observations only make sense within a complex framework of existing facts and theories which have been accumulated and developed through many centuries. You only know what you do about the moon and the stars because of a long and complex cultural history (a small part of which is told in Chapter 2), which mediates between the light from the night sky and your thoughts about astronomy and cosmology. That history includes the successful challenging of the old earth-centred world view by Galileo Galilei, with the help of Copernicus's astronomy and the newly invented telescope in the early 17th century, as well as the establishment of Newton's laws of motion and gravitation later in that century, and more recent developments in physics and cosmology too. It also includes, crucially, the histories of those social and political mechanisms that allow for, and control, the dissemination of scientific knowledge among the people through books and in classrooms.

We should also notice, by the way, that what science often aims to show is that things in themselves are not as they initially seem to us – that appearances can be deceptive. The earth beneath our feet certainly seems to be solid and stable, and the sun and the other stars appear to move around us. But science eventually showed that, despite all the sensory evidence to the contrary, the earth is not only spinning on its own axis but is also hurtling around the sun at great speed. Indeed, one of the characters in Galileo's *Dialogue Concerning the Two Chief World Systems* (1632) expresses his admiration on just these grounds for those who, like Aristarchus and Copernicus, had been able to believe in the sun-centred system before the advent of the telescope: 'I cannot sufficiently admire the intellectual eminence of those who received it and held it to be true. They have by sheer force of intellect done such violence to their own senses as to prefer what reason told them over that which sense experience plainly showed them to be the case.' In more recent times, both evolutionary biology and quantum mechanics have similarly required people to believe the most implausible things – that we share an ancestor not only with rabbits but also with carrots, for example, or that the smallest components of matter are simultaneously both waves and particles. People sometimes say that science is just a systematization of empirical observations, or nothing more than the careful application of common sense. However, it also has the ambition and the potential to show that our senses deceive us and that our basic intuitions may lead us astray.

But when you look up at the night sky, you may not be thinking about astronomy and cosmology at all. You may instead be gripped by a sense of the power of nature, the beauty and grandeur of the heavens, the vastness of space and time, and your own smallness and insignificance. This might even be a religious experience for you, reinforcing your feeling of awe at the power of God and the immensity and complexity of his creation, putting you in mind of the words of Psalm 19: 'The heavens declare the glory of God; the skies proclaim the work of his hands.'

Such an emotional and religious response to the night sky would, of course, be every bit as historically and culturally mediated as the experience of perceiving the moon and the stars in terms of modern cosmology. Without some kind of religious education you certainly would not be able to quote from the Bible, and you would perhaps not even be able to formulate a developed concept of God. Individual religious experiences, like modern scientific observations, are made possible by long processes of human collaboration in a shared quest for understanding. In the religious case, what intervenes between the light hitting your retina and your thoughts about the glory of God is the lengthy history of a particular sacred text, and its reading and interpretation within a succession of human communities. And, as in the scientific case, one of the lessons learned through that communal endeavour is that things are not as they seem. Religious teachers, as much as scientific ones, try to show their pupils that there is an unseen world behind the observed one – and one which might overturn their most settled intuitions and beliefs.

The political dimension

Among historians of science and religion there have been two interestingly different kinds of attack on the 'conflict narrative' favoured by Enlightenment rationalists, Victorian freethinkers, and modern-day scientific atheists. The first strategy is to replace the overarching image of conflict with that of complexity, and to put emphasis on the very different ways that science–religion interactions have developed at different times, in different places, and in different local circumstances. Some scientists have been religious, others atheists. Some religious denominations welcome modern science, others are suspicious of it. Recognizing that neither 'science' nor 'religion' refers to a simple singular entity is an important part of this approach too, as is acknowledging the existence of considerable national differences. To take just the most obvious example, debates about evolution and religion have, from the beginning of the 20th century and right up to the present day, developed quite differently in the United States than they have in Europe and elsewhere. As I will explain in Chapter 5, the debates about the teaching of evolution in schools that go on in America today emerged through circumstances very specific to that country, most importantly the interpretation of the First Amendment to its Constitution, which prohibits the government from passing any law 'respecting an establishment of religion'.

If this first approach to the conflict narrative is to change the plot, the second involves recasting the leading characters. This approach says: yes, there have been conflicts that seem to be between science and religion, and they are real conflicts, but they are not between science and religion. The question then is: who or what are the real antagonists in this story? In a way, we are then just straight back into the messy details of historical complexity. There is certainly not a simple recasting that works for all cases, but the general idea is that the real conflict is a political one about the production and dissemination of knowledge. The opposition of science versus religion is then seen to be standing proxy for some classic modern political conflicts: the individual versus the state, or secular liberalism versus conservative traditionalism. It is interesting to note that in modern America, for example, campaigners both for and against the teaching of evolution in schools have portrayed themselves as representing the rights and freedoms of the people against an intolerant and authoritarian establishment which is controlling the educational agenda. In the 1920s that establishment was portrayed by defenders of evolution as Christian and conservative, but to some religious groups today it seems that a secular liberal elite have taken control of the education system. Debates about science and religion give certain groups an opportunity to argue their case for greater social influence, and greater control over the mechanisms of state education, a case that rests on quite independent political grounds.

These questions about the politics of knowledge will arise repeatedly in subsequent chapters. For the moment, let us consider just one other example – the philosopher and firebrand Thomas Paine. An unsuccessful corset-maker, sacked tax-collector, and occasional political writer, Paine left his native England to start a new life in America in 1774. On his arrival in Philadelphia, he found work as the editor of the *Pennsylvania Magazine*. A couple of years later, his polemical pamphlet *Common Sense* (1776) was a key factor in persuading the American colonists to go to war against the British government, and established Paine as the bestselling author of the age. An associate of Benjamin Rush, Thomas Jefferson, and others of the founding fathers of the United States of America, Paine's democratic and anti-monarchical political philosophy shaped the Declaration of Independence. After politics, Paine's other great passions were science and engineering. He had attended popular lectures on Newton and astronomy back in England, and he spent many years of his life working on a design for a single-span iron bridge, inspired by the delicacy and strength of one of the great works of nature – the spider's web. His whole philosophy was a scientific one. He saw revolutions in governments paralleling the revolutions of celestial bodies in the heavens. Each was an inevitable, natural, and law-governed process. Later in his life, having had a hand in both the American and French revolutions, he turned his sights from monarchy to Christianity. The institutions of Christianity were as offensive to his enlightened and Newtonian sensibilities as were those of monarchical government. In his *Age of Reason* (1794), Paine complained of 'the continual persecution carried on by the Church, for several hundred years, against the sciences and against the professors of science'.

Paine's version of the conflict narrative makes most sense when seen in its political context. Paine was, indeed, a scientific thinker who was opposed to Christianity. He denounced the Bible, especially the Old Testament, with its stories of 'voluptuous debaucheries' among the Israelites and the 'unrelenting vindictiveness' of their God. To the shock of his friends, Paine wrote of the Bible: 'I sincerely detest it, as I detest everything that is cruel.' Paine also lambasted the 'priestcraft' at work in the 'adulterous' relationship between the Church of England and the British state. What he hoped for, though, was not an end to religion but the replacement of Christian religion by a rational religion based on the study of nature – one which recognized the existence of God, the importance of morality, and the hope for a future life, but did away with scriptures, priests, and the authority of the state. His reasons for this were democratic ones. National churches lorded illegitimate power over the people by claiming special access to divine truths and revelations. But everyone can read the book of nature and understand the goodness, power, and generosity of its author. In the religion of Deism recommended by Paine, there was no need for the people to be in thrall either to priests or to the state. Science could help to replace Christianity by showing that every individual could find God by looking at the night sky rather than by reading the Bible or going to church. 'That which is now called natural philosophy', Paine wrote, 'embracing the whole circle of science of which astronomy occupies the chief place, is the study of the works of God, and of the power and wisdom of God and his works, and is the true theology.'

Paine's democratic ideals, including the separation of church and state, are enshrined in the founding documents of the United States. And in modern America too, it is competing political visions that come into conflict in debates about science and religion. American politicians who deny the truth of the theory of evolution and advocate the teaching of a religiously motivated concept of 'Intelligent Design' in schools do not do so for scientific reasons. They do so, rather, to send a signal – to indicate their general support for Christianity, their opposition to excessively secularist interpretations of the Constitution, and their hostility to naturalistic and materialistic world views.

A final interesting piece of support for the suggestion that what is really at stake in science–religion encounters is politics, is to be found in two mid-20th-century stage plays. Each dramatizes a famous clash between a heroic scientific individual and a reactionary and authoritarian religious establishment, and does so to make primarily political points. Bertolt Brecht's *Life of Galileo* was composed during the 1930s and early 1940s. Brecht was a German communist, opposed to fascism, and living in exile in Denmark and subsequently the United States. The play uses the story of Galileo to investigate the dilemmas faced by a dissident intellectual living under a repressive regime, and also to suggest the importance of pursuing scientific knowledge for moral and social ends rather than purely for its own sake. Brecht saw in the well-known Galileo affair political lessons which could be applied to a world struggling against authoritarian fascism and, in the later version of the play, living in the shadow of the dropping of atomic bombs on Hiroshima and Nagasaki.

Jerome Lawrence and Robert E. Lee's play *Inherit the Wind*, first performed in 1955, and made into a famous film in 1960, was a dramatization of the Scopes 'monkey trial' of 1925. The historical events on which the play was based are discussed in Chapter 5; they centre on the prosecution of a Tennessee school teacher, John Scopes, for teaching evolution in contravention of state law. *Inherit the Wind* used the Scopes case to attack the anti-communist purges of the McCarthy era. Scopes, the heroic evolutionist standing up against a repressive Christian establishment in 1920s Tennessee, stood for the struggle for freedom of opinion, association, and expression by communist sympathizers in the face of a repressive American government machine. Among those sympathizers, incidentally, was Bertolt Brecht, who had been called to testify before the House Committee on Un-American Activities in 1947. In the case both of Brecht's *Galileo* and Lawrence and Lee's *Inherit the Wind*, it was questions of intellectual freedom, political power, and human morality that gave the conflict between science and religion its drama and its interest. The same is true in real life.

'Science and religion' as an academic field

So far we have looked at science and religion in general terms as two cultural enterprises which encounter each other both in the mind of the individual and in the political domain. There is an important further dimension to add to this preliminary picture, which is the recent development of 'science and religion' as an academic field in its own right.

Of course theologians, philosophers, and scientists have been writing treatises about the relationship between natural knowledge and revelation for centuries. Many of these works were very popular, especially in the 18th and 19th centuries. The most famous was *Natural Theology* (1802) by the Anglican clergyman William Paley, which argued from the complex adaptations of plants and animals to the existence of an intelligent designer. However, from the 1960s onwards 'science and religion' took on a more distinct existence as an academic discipline. In 1966 the first specialist journal in the field was founded in Chicago – *Zygon: Journal of Religion and Science*. The same year saw the publication of a very widely used textbook, *Issues in Science and Religion* by the British physicist and theologian Ian Barbour. Since that time, various organizations have been set up to foster this kind of work, including a European Society for the Study of Science and Theology, and an International Society for Science and Religion. There are established academic posts devoted specifically to the study of science and religion at several major institutions, including the universities of Oxford and Cambridge in the UK, and Princeton Theological Seminary in the US.

Academic work by scientists and theologians seeking to develop a harmonious interdisciplinary dialogue has been supported by a range of institutions, including the Roman Catholic Church, through the work of the Vatican Observatory, and also the John Templeton Foundation in America – a philanthropic organization particularly committed to supporting research that harmonizes science with religion. A recent large Templeton-funded project has been devoted to research on altruism and 'unlimited love', for example. One outcome of this has been a book explaining the improved physical health and mental well-being enjoyed by those who live an altruistic and compassionate life.

The John Templeton Foundation spends millions of dollars on research grants each year, including an annual Templeton Prize, currently valued at about $1.5 million, given to an individual

14

for 'Progress Toward Research or Discoveries about Spiritual Realities'. Former winners have included Christian evangelists, leading figures from non-Christian faiths, and also many individuals who have been prominent in the academic dialogue between science and religion, such as Ian Barbour, Arthur Peacocke, John Polkinghorne, Paul Davies, and George Ellis. Like many of those who have contributed to the creation of 'science and religion' as an academic subject, all of the figures just named fall into the category of religiously committed professional scientists (and in some cases ordained ministers). There are also many historians, philosophers, and theologians who have contributed significantly to the field. It is a topic that even attracts impassioned contributions from scientific atheists, such as Oxford University's Professor for the Public Understanding of Science, Richard Dawkins.

I have already mentioned that much academic work in this area has been concerned with the plausibility (or lack of it) of the idea of an inevitable conflict between science and religion. This concern is partly driven by apologetic motives. Many of those involved in the field are religious believers committed to showing that science need not undermine faith. But the denial of conflict (or of any other one-dimensional relationship) is also motivated by more purely academic considerations, several of which will emerge in subsequent chapters.

Whether arguing for conflict or for harmony, it could be objected that any talk about 'the relationship between science and religion' obscures the true plurality and complexity of the terms. 'Science' and 'religion' are both hazy categories with blurry boundaries, and different sciences and different religions have clearly related to each other in different ways. Mathematics and astronomy were both particularly nurtured in Islamic cultures in the Middle Ages, for example, where they were used to calculate the correct times of prayer and the direction of Mecca, as well as for many more secular purposes. Islamic scholars working in academies such as the House of Wisdom in Baghdad preserved, tested, and improved upon ancient Greek medicine and optics, as well as astronomy and astrology, between the 9th and the 15th centuries. The motto of these scholars was: 'Whoever does not know astronomy and anatomy is deficient in the knowledge of God.' Their works were to be crucial sources for the revival of European learning from the later Middle Ages onwards.

Excluded from more mainstream European academic institutions, Jewish communities formed a particularly strong connection with the science and practice of medicine in early modern Europe. The Roman Catholic Church, despite the high-profile difficulties caused by Galileo's ideas, was one of the most generous sponsors of scientific research during the Renaissance, especially through the investment of the Jesuit order in astronomical observatories and experimental equipment. The relationship between modern scientific knowledge – a characteristically Western system of thought – and the religious traditions of the East, is different again. Here we might think of the interest shown by Buddhists in neuroscientific studies of the state of the brain during meditation, or of Fritjof Capra's 1975 bestseller, *The Tao of Physics: An Exploration of the Parallels between Modern Physics and Eastern Mysticism*. There is, finally, a very particular story to be told about the relationship between evolutionary biology and modern Protestant Christianity – one which we will return to below. The point is that none of these particular relationships can serve as a universal template for understanding engagements between science and religion.

Some think that the extent of oversimplification, generalization, and reification involved in even using the phrase 'science and religion' makes it a non-starter as a sensible topic for academic study. I have some sympathy with this view. It is certainly true that in this book, as in most contributions to the field, the 'religion' under discussion is most often specifically Christianity. However, at least within the Abrahamic, monotheistic traditions of Judaism,

Christianity, and Islam, there is enough common ground, historically, philosophically, and theologically, for a more general discussion to take place. Whether it is possible or desirable to extend that discussion still further to include non-theistic or non-scriptural traditions is another question, and one which I will not explore further here. The monotheistic faiths, however, are all united by the idea that God is the author of two books – the book of nature and the book of scripture – and that the individual believer will find their understanding and their faith strengthened through the careful reading of both books. The intellectual, political, and ethical implications of that shared commitment to reading God's words and his works have developed in comparable, although far from identical, ways in the three major monotheistic traditions.

The fact that the phrase 'science and religion' names an academic field, as well as conjuring up vivid if historically debatable cultural stereotypes, is enough, I think, to justify its continued use as a category of thought (and in the title of this and many other books). Academics and journalists alike continue to write as if there were some ongoing general relationship between science and religion, in terms of which particular contemporary episodes might be understood. Even if that relationship really exists only in our imaginations, it is still important to try to understand how it got there. Since Galileo Galilei and his encounter with the Roman Inquisition takes centre stage in many popular accounts of that relationship, his story is an appropriate place to start our inquiry.

Chapter 2
Galileo and the philosophy of science

When Galileo recanted his Copernicanism in 1633, what did that signify? Was it a victory for religious obscurantism and a defeat for free scientific inquiry? Was it evidence that science and religion are inevitably locked in ideological and institutional combat? Unsurprisingly, there was more to it than that. On all sides of the Galileo case there was agreement that it was proper and rational both to seek accurate knowledge of the world through observation of nature and also to base one's beliefs on the Bible. The conflict was not between empirical science and authoritarian religion but rather between differing views within the Catholic Church about how to interpret nature and scripture, especially when they seemed to disagree. An appreciation of the exact context of Galileo's trial, the shadow cast over it by the Protestant Reformation of the previous century, and the politics of the Papal court at the time all help to explain how these issues took on the dramatic character that they did in 1633, almost a century after Nicolaus Copernicus had argued for a sun-centred astronomy in his book *On the Revolutions of the Heavenly Spheres* in 1543.

Before coming back to this retelling of the Galileo story as a disagreement among 17th-century Catholics about how to read the Bible, it will be useful to look at some general questions about the sources of knowledge. These will help to make sense both of what was at stake in Rome in June 1633 and also of general questions about the philosophy of science that frequently recur in contemporary debates about science and religion.

How do we know anything?

We generally derive our knowledge of the world from four sources: our senses, our powers of rational thought, the testimony of others, and our memory. The first obvious thing to note about all these sources is that they are fallible. Our senses can deceive us, our reasoning can be faulty, other people can knowingly or accidentally mislead us, and most of us know only too well (and increasingly with age) how partial and distorted our memories can be. The whole project of modern science could be summarized as the attempt to weave these individually relatively feeble threads into a more resilient web of knowledge. So the sense experience of one person must be witnessed, corroborated, and repeated by many others before it is accepted. Simple observations of the properties of things must be supplemented by carefully designed experiments which test more precisely how they behave in different circumstances. Human powers of perception on their own may be limited, but the invention of the telescope and the microscope in the early 17th century, and of many other even more sophisticated devices since then, has enormously increased the scope and accuracy of the observations and measurements that can be made. But experiments could not be designed, and observations would not make any sense, without the use of reason. Theoretical hypotheses about the nature of reality, and reasoning about what experimental evidence is needed to support or refute them, are prerequisites of scientific knowledge. Finally, scientific experts must cite the sources of their knowledge and explain the chain of their reasoning if their testimony is to be accepted. And the publication of scientific results in treatises, books, specialist journals, and, now, electronic databases provides us with a collective and well-documented memory greater than anything that would be possible by relying on one person's memory alone.

The knowledge thus produced is a highly prized possession in human societies. It bestows on us the ability to manipulate not only the natural world but also each other. One of the most important advocates of science in 17th-century England, Francis Bacon, wrote that 'human knowledge and human power meet in one; for where the cause is not known the effect cannot be produced'. In other words, an understanding of the secret workings of nature would allow people to produce machines and medicines to improve the human condition. Bacon also wrote, to justify the new knowledge of the period, that 'all knowledge appeareth to be a plant of God's own planting', whose spread and flourishing at that time had been divinely ordained.

Natural philosophers in 17th-century England such as Robert Boyle and Robert Hooke – the new 'virtuosi' of the experimental method, the founders of the Royal Society – were perceived by some as a threat to orthodoxy. Their claims to be able both to discover and to manipulate hidden forces in nature seemed to verge on usurping the role of God. That was why it was important to reassure their readers that in reaping this knowledge they were collecting a harvest which was, in Bacon's words, 'of God's own planting'. In this image, God planted the seed of knowledge and natural philosophers harvested its fruit. According to another popular metaphor, God was imagined not as a kind of cosmic farmer but, as we have noted, as an author of two books – the book of nature and the book of scripture. This metaphor was based on the same idea – that the ultimate source of knowledge was God and that humans had to adopt certain techniques to acquire that knowledge.

One of the useful things about these metaphors of agriculture and of reading is that they draw attention to the fact that human knowledge (at least of the natural kind) is made rather than simply found. Seeds do not become plants and bear fruit unless they are sown in the right conditions, are watered and fed, and are harvested in the right way. Texts do not generally have obvious meanings, but rather these must be teased out through the collective efforts of many readers using different historical and literary techniques. Even if one decides to approach a text in search of its 'literal' meaning, that is by no means a simple matter. It is also well known among literary scholars that the project of discerning an author's intentions in a text is a difficult and controversial one. The histories of science and religion reveal that these difficulties have been experienced in full measure in relation to both of God's books. Neither nature nor scripture offers a transparent account of its author's intentions. Some have gone further, of course, and denied that either is a work of divine authorship at all. Some read the book of nature as an autobiography and the scriptures as purely human works.

This brings us to the question of whether, in addition to the four sources of knowledge already mentioned – sense, reason, testimony, and memory – a fifth needs to be added, namely revelation. It is a belief shared by Jews, Christians, and Muslims that God's authorship can be detected both in nature and in scripture (the Torah, the Bible, or the Quran, respectively). While the natural world reveals the power, intelligence, and goodness of its Creator, the scriptures reveal God's plans for his chosen people and the legal and moral basis according to which they should live. Corresponding to this idea is the subtly different distinction between natural and revealed forms of knowledge. Natural knowledge is produced by the exercise of the natural human faculties of sense and reason (these faculties can be engaged in reasoning about scripture as well as about the natural world). Revealed knowledge is produced by a supernatural uncovering of the truth – either through the medium of scripture or by a direct revelation of God to the individual believer. Natural theology, then, as opposed to revealed theology, is a form of discourse about God based on human reason rather than on revelation. This includes theological works making inferences about God from the design apparent in the natural world – as in William Paley's famous *Natural Theology* (1802) – but it also includes more purely philosophical works about God's existence and attributes. Modern books arguing for belief in 'Intelligent Design' on the basis of the 'irreducible complexity' of nature are within this same tradition, as we will see in Chapter 5.

Debates about science and religion virtually always involve disagreements about the relative authority of different sources of knowledge. This is true of debates about the relative weight to be given to testimony and to experience when considering claims about miracles, as we will see in Chapter 3. It is also true of the 18th-century clash between Deism and Christianity. Thomas Paine's objection to Christian philosophers was not that they found God in nature – he did too – but that they thought they could also find God through his self-revelation in the Bible. For Paine, the only possible kind of revelation was from God directly to an individual. If God ever did act in this way, it was revelation 'to the first person only, and hearsay to every other'. The scriptures were therefore no more than mere human testimony and the rational reader was not obliged to believe them. Advocates of creationism in the 20th century took the opposite approach to Paine's. For them, the word of God as revealed in the Bible was the most reliable form of knowledge and anything that seemed to contradict their interpretation of scripture had to be rejected. This included mainstream scientific theories of evolution. Some creationists were even moved to re-read the book of nature and produce their own 'Creation Science' which harmonized geology with Genesis. While rationalists have rejected revelation altogether, and fundamentalists have insisted that all forms of knowledge be tested against the Bible, many more have looked for ways to reconcile their readings of God's two books without doing violence to either.

The rise and fall of Galileo

Galileo belonged to this last category of believers seeking harmony between the Bible and knowledge of nature. He endorsed the view that the Bible is about how to go to heaven and not about how the heavens go. In other words, if you wanted to know about matters pertaining to salvation you should consult scripture, but if you were interested in the detailed workings of the natural world, then there were better starting points – namely empirical observations and reasoned demonstrations. This was not a particularly unorthodox view in itself, but Galileo failed to persuade the authorities that it was a principle that could be applied to his case. Although the church was certainly not opposed in general to the study of mathematics, astronomy, and the other sciences, there were limits to how far the authority of the Bible and of the church could be challenged by an individual layman like Galileo. He went beyond those limits. There were three central characters in the story of how he did so – the telescope, the Bible, and Pope Urban VIII.

At the beginning of the 17th century, Galileo was one of only a tiny handful of natural philosophers who thought it likely that the Copernican astronomy was an accurate description of the universe. The majority of those who took an interest in such questions, including the mathematicians and astronomers working within the Roman Catholic Church, held to the system of physics and cosmology associated with the ancient Greek philosopher Aristotle. There were two elements in this existing Aristotelian science which would be challenged by Galileo. First, there was the earth-centred model of the cosmos produced by the 2nd-century Greek astronomer Ptolemy. This was the standard astronomical model and, despite certain complexities and technical problems, it worked as well as the Copernican model as a device for calculating the positions of the stars and planets, and had the considerable advantage of according with the common-sense intuition that the earth was not in motion. The second Aristotelian principle that would come under attack was the division of the cosmos into two regions – the sublunary and the superlunary. The sublunary region consisted of everything within the orbit of the moon. This was the region of corruption

2. A 16th-century illustration of Ptolemy's earth-centred astronomical system. At the centre is the world, composed of the four elements of earth, water, air, and fire, surrounded by the spheres of the moon, Mercury, Venus, the sun, Mars, Jupiter, Saturn, and finally the sphere of the fixed stars. This Ptolemaic system had been endorsed by Aristotle and was still accepted by almost all natural philosophers at the start of the 17th century.

and imperfection and of the four elements of earth, water, air, and fire. In the superlunary region, the domain of all the celestial bodies, everything was composed of a fifth element, ether, and was characterized by perfect circular motion.

Galileo's great contribution to astronomy was to use a newly invented optical instrument – named the 'telescope' in 1611 – to provide observations with which to challenge this Aristotelian and

Ptolemaic theory. Galileo did not invent the telescope himself, but as soon as he heard of its invention he set about making his own superior version. The earliest telescopes, made in the Netherlands, magnified only by a factor of three. Galileo developed an instrument with magnifying power of about twenty times, which he turned towards the heavens with spectacular results. These results were published in two books, *The Starry Messenger* in 1610 and his *Letters on Sunspots* in 1613, which established his reputation as a brilliant observational astronomer and as one of the leading natural philosophers in Europe. These works also made it clear that Galileo favoured the Copernican astronomy.

Just a couple of examples will give a sense of how Galileo wielded his telescope against Aristotelian science. Perhaps the most telling single discovery made by Galileo was that Venus, when viewed through the telescope, could be seen to display phases. In other words, like the moon, its apparent shape varied between a small crescent and a full disc. This strongly suggested that Venus orbited the sun. If the Ptolemaic system had been true and Venus, which was known always to be close to the sun in the sky, described an orbit closer to the earth than the sun's, then it should have appeared always as a thin crescent. Secondly, Galileo was able to deploy a number of key observations against the strong commitment of the Aristotelians to the division of the cosmos into distinct sublunary and superlunary regions. His telescope revealed that the moon was a rocky satellite with craters and mountains – more like the earth than like an ethereal and perfect heavenly body. He also showed that Jupiter had four satellites or moons. This helped defeat a common objection to the Copernican theory. On the Ptolemaic theory, the earth's moon was treated as the closest of several planets, all of whose orbits centred on the earth. If Copernicus were right, then the moon would have to orbit the earth, while the earth in turn went around the sun. Was it possible that a celestial body could move in an orbit with a centre other than the centre of the cosmos? The discovery that Jupiter was accompanied in its orbit (whether that was around the earth or around the sun) by four satellites established that such motion was indeed possible. Finally, Galileo's discovery of sunspots further undermined the Aristotelian distinction between perfect heavenly bodies and a changeable and imperfect earth.

It was largely thanks to Galileo's publications that Copernicanism became such a live issue in the 1610s. Galileo was aware that his advocacy of the new astronomy was arousing both theological and scientific objections. One of the reasons for the former was the apparent inconsistency between Copernican astronomy and the Bible. Several Old Testament passages referred to the movement of the sun through the heavens and the immobility of the earth. An often-quoted passage was from the Book of Joshua, which referred to God stopping the sun and the moon in the sky to light the earth while the Israelites took vengeance on the Amorites. Seeking to forestall biblical objections to the view that the earth moves, Galileo wrote his *Letter to the Grand Duchess Christina* in 1615 in which he articulated his views about how to deal with apparent conflicts between natural and revealed knowledge. He relied heavily on the views of the Fathers of the Catholic Church, especially St Augustine. The central idea was the principle of accommodation. This stated that the Bible was written in language accommodated to the limited knowledge of the relatively uneducated people to whom it was initially revealed. Since the readers of the Book of Joshua believed that the earth was stationary and the sun moved around it, God's word was couched in terms that they would understand. All agreed that biblical references to God's 'right hand' or to God's experience of human passions such as anger should not be taken literally but were accommodations to common understanding. Galileo argued that the same attitude should be taken to biblical passages referring to the movement of the sun. The other general principle Galileo adopted, mentioned above, was that the Bible should only be given priority in matters relating to salvation. In matters of natural knowledge, if the text seemed to contradict the best available science, then it would need to be reinterpreted.

All of this was indeed in tune with St Augustine's 4th-century approach to scripture. However, Galileo was writing at a time when more conservative views were in the ascendancy thanks to the crisis of the Protestant Reformation, which had started in the early decades of the 16th century in Germany and England, and continued to divide Europe both politically and religiously in the 17th century. One of the central tenets of Protestant forms of Christianity was the importance of scripture and the right of each individual to read the Bible in their own language, rather than encountering Christian teaching only through the mediation of priests and the doctrinal pronouncements of Church Councils. The Catholic Church's principal response to the Reformation came in the form of a series of meetings which comprised the Council of Trent (1545–63). One of the declarations of that Council was that, in matters of faith and morals,

> no one, relying on his own judgement and distorting the Sacred
> Scriptures according to his own conceptions, shall dare to interpret
> them contrary to that sense which Holy Mother Church, to whom
> it belongs to judge their true sense and meaning, has held and does
> hold, or even contrary to the unanimous agreement of the Fathers.

In the context of these Counter-Reformation teachings, Galileo's suggestion in his *Letter to the Grand Duchess Christina* that he, an individual layman, had the authority to tell the 'Holy Mother Church' which parts of scripture needed to be reinterpreted, and how, smacked both of arrogance and of dangerous Protestant leanings. The fact that in 1632 he would publish his *Dialogue* in vernacular Italian rather than scholarly Latin would add further to that impression.

When a committee was asked to report on the question of Copernicanism to the Inquisition in 1616, it declared it to be both false and absurd as scientific doctrine, and additionally to be contrary to the teachings of scripture and thus formally heretical. Galileo was personally summoned into the presence of Cardinal

Robert Bellarmine, who instructed him that he must not hold or defend the Copernican astronomy. At the same time, Copernicus's *On the Revolutions of the Heavenly Spheres*, which had been largely ignored since its appearance in print, was now suspended from publication, pending 'correction'. By drawing new attention to Copernicanism and to the Church's attitude to scripture, Galileo had succeeded in having the former declared heretical and in seeing the latter hardened and entrenched in a more conservative position.

The election in 1623 of Cardinal Maffeo Barberini as Pope Urban VIII must have seemed to Galileo like the answer to his prayers. Barberini was an educated and cultured Florentine. Even better, since 1611 he had been an admirer and active supporter of Galileo's work, even composing a poem, *Adulatio Perniciosa* ('In Dangerous Adulation') in 1620, expressing his admiration for Galileo's telescopic discoveries. In 1624, Galileo had several meetings with Urban VIII, during which he was assured that he could discuss the Copernican theory in his work but only as one hypothesis among others. Urban argued that God, in his omnipotence, could make the heavens move in any way he wished, and so it would be presumptuous to claim to have discovered the precise manner in which this end was achieved by the divine will. Galileo nevertheless left Rome reassured and was soon at work on the book that would be published in 1632 as his *Dialogue Concerning the Two Chief World Systems*.

This was when the real trouble started. Although the *Dialogue* was presented as an even-handed discussion among three characters – an Aristotelian, a Copernican, and a common-sensical everyman – it was perfectly clear to most readers that the arguments given in favour of the Copernican system were very much stronger than those made in defence of the old earth-centred astronomy, and that Galileo had in effect produced a pro-Copernican piece of propaganda, thus breaching the conditions of the 1616 injunction and the instructions given by

3. Maffeo Barberini, Pope Urban VIII, painted by Gian Lorenzo
Bernini in 1632, the year that Galileo's *Dialogue* was published, in
which the Pope's views were put in the mouth of the Aristotelian
philosopher Simplicio

Urban in 1624. That was not all. The Aristotelian character was named 'Simplicio'. This was the name of a 6th-century Aristotelian philosopher but also one that hinted at simple-mindedness. Even more provocatively, one of the arguments put forward by simple Simplicio was the one that had been put to Galileo by Urban himself in 1624 – namely that God could have produced natural effects in any way he chose, and so it was wrong to claim necessary truth for any given physical hypothesis about their causation. This apparent mockery of the Pope added personal insult to the already grave injury delivered by Galileo's disobedience. And the timing could not have been worse. The *Dialogue* arrived in Rome in 1632 at a moment of great political crisis. Urban was in the midst of switching his allegiance from the French to the Spanish during the Thirty Years War and was in no mood for leniency. He needed to show his new conservative allies that he was a decisive and authoritative defender of the faith. So Galileo was summoned to Rome to be tried before the Inquisition.

As with the Scopes trial in America three centuries later, the trial of Galileo in 1633 was one in which the outcome was never in doubt. Galileo was found guilty of promoting the heretical Copernican view in contravention of the express injunction not to do so that he had received in 1616. It was for disobeying the Church, rather than for seeking to understand the natural world through observation and reasoning, that Galileo was condemned. Galileo's political misjudgement of his relationship with Pope Urban VIII played as much of a role in his downfall as did his over-reaching of himself in the field of biblical interpretation. Galileo's work was to be one key contribution to the eventual success of the Copernican theory, which, when modified by further scientific insights such as Kepler's replacement of circular by elliptical orbits, and Newton's discovery of the law of gravitation, was virtually universally accepted. However, in 1632 there was sufficient doubt about the relative merits of the Copernican system and the alternatives (including Tycho Brahe's compromise according to which the sun orbited the earth but all the other planets orbited the sun) that an objective observer would have pronounced the scientific question an open one, making it even harder to decide how to judge between the teachings that the Church declared to be contained in the book of scripture and those which Galileo had read through his telescope in the book of nature.

Appearance and reality

Historians have shown that the Galileo affair, remembered by some as a clash between science and religion, was primarily a dispute about the enduring political question of who was authorized to produce and disseminate knowledge. In the world of Counter-Reformation Rome, in the midst of the Thirty Years War, which continued to pit the Protestant and Catholic powers of Europe against each other, Galileo's claim to be able to settle questions about competing sources of knowledge through his own individual reading and reasoning seemed the height of presumption and a direct threat to the authority of the Church.

The case can also be used to illustrate one further philosophical question that has been central to modern debates about science and religion, namely the issue of realism. Arguments about realism particularly arise in connection with what scientific theories have to say about unobservable entities such as magnetic fields, black holes, electrons, quarks, superstrings, and the like. To be a realist is to suppose that science is in the business of providing accurate descriptions of such entities. To be an anti-realist is to remain agnostic about the accuracy of such descriptions and to hold that science is in the business only of providing accurate predictions of observable phenomena. Urban VIII was not alone among theologians and philosophers in the 16th and 17th centuries in taking an anti-realist or 'instrumentalist' approach to astronomy. On that view, the Ptolemaic and Copernican systems could be used to calculate and predict the apparent motions of the stars and planets, but there was no way to know which system, if either, represented the way that God had in fact chosen to structure the heavens. Indeed, when Copernicus's *On the Revolutions of the Heavenly Spheres* was first published, it had attached to it a preface written by the Lutheran Andreas Osiander stating that the theory was intended purely as a calculating device rather than as a physical description.

Galileo, on the other hand, took a realist attitude – indeed, it was his insistence on arguing the case for the physical reality of the sun-centred system which resulted in his trial before the Inquisition. Galileo was a member of one of the earliest scientific societies, the Academy of Lynxes, founded in 1603 by Prince Cesi. The lynx was thought to be able to see in the dark and so to perceive things invisible to others. Using new scientific instruments such as the telescope and the microscope in conjunction with the power of reason and the language of mathematics, Galileo and his fellow 'lynxes' aimed not just to find useful models for predicting observable phenomena but explanations of those phenomena in terms of the invisible structures and forces of the universe. They seemed to be succeeding. In addition to Galileo's telescopic and astronomical discoveries, the microscope was opening up a different kind of previously unseen world. Using an instrument sent to him by Galileo, Prince Cesi made the first known microscopic observations in the 1620s. Cesi's observations of bees were recorded in engravings by Francesco Stelluti and used as a device to seek approval for the Academy of Lynxes from Urban VIII, whose family coat of arms featured three large bees.

Debates between realists and anti-realists continue to form a lively and fascinating part of the philosophy of science. Each side rests on a very plausible intuition. The realist intuition is that our sense impressions are caused by an external world that exists and has properties independently of human observers, so that it is reasonable to try to discover what those properties are, whether the entities in question are directly observable by us or

4. Francesco Stelluti's *Melissographia* (1625), produced using a microscope provided by Galileo, and dedicated to Pope Urban VIII

not. The anti-realist intuition is that all we ever discover, either individually or collectively, is how the world appears to us. We live in an endless series of mental impressions, which we can never compare with the nature of things in themselves. We cannot, even for an instant, draw back the veil of phenomena to check whether our descriptions of reality are right. We can have no knowledge of the world beyond the impression it makes on us, and so, the anti-realist concludes, we should remain agnostic about the hidden forces and structures which scientists hypothesize about in their attempts to explain those impressions.

Modern debates about scientific realism have centred on the question of the success of science. Realists argue that the success of scientific theories – quantum physics, for instance – that posit unobservable entities in explaining physical phenomena, in intervening in nature to produce new effects, and in providing ever more detailed and accurate predictions, would be a miracle unless those entities, such as electrons, actually existed and had the properties scientists ascribed to them. Anti-realists have a couple of good responses to this. First, they can point out that the history of science is a graveyard of now-abandoned theories which were once the most successful available but which posited entities we now do not believe existed. This would apply to the 18th-century theory of combustion, according to which a substance known as 'phlogiston' was given off when things burned. Another example is the 'ether' of 19th-century physics – a physical medium that was supposed to be necessary for the propagation of electromagnetic waves. Since theories we now take to be untrue have made successful predictions in the past (including also Ptolemaic astronomy, which was hugely successful for many centuries), there is no reason to suppose that today's successful theories are true. Both true and untrue theories can produce accurate empirical predictions.

A second anti-realist argument was put forward by two influential philosophers of science in the 20th century – Thomas Kuhn and Bas van Fraassen. Kuhn's book, *The Structure of Scientific Revolutions*, first published in 1962, has become a classic in the field and one of the most widely read books about scientific knowledge. The book focused on what Kuhn called 'paradigm shifts' in the history of science, when one dominant world view was replaced by another, as in the case of Copernican astronomy replacing the Ptolemaic theory, or Einsteinian physics replacing pure Newtonianism. Kuhn portrayed scientific progress as a Darwinian process of variation and selection. He did not think that the improved accuracy and predictive power of later theories showed that they had progressed further towards true descriptions of reality, but rather that they had been chosen by the scientific community from among the various proposed theories because of their improved instrumental power and puzzle-solving ability. Bas van Fraassen, in his 1980 book *The Scientific Image*, also made use of this 'Darwinian' explanation of the success of science. Since scientists will discard theories that make false predictions (as nature discards non-adaptive variations) and keep hold of those that make successful predictions, he argued, the fact that as time goes on their predictions get better is no surprise at all, let alone a miracle. They were selected for precisely that instrumental success, and there is no need for a further appeal to unobservable realities to explain that success.

Science and religion have a shared concern with the relationship between the observable and the unobservable. The Nicene Creed includes the statement that God made 'all that is, seen and unseen'. St Paul wrote in his letter to the Romans that 'since the creation of the world God's invisible qualities – his eternal power and divine nature – have been clearly seen, being understood from what has been made'. However, there are anti-realists among theologians too. The intuition here is similar to that of the scientific anti-realist. We have no way (at least not yet) to check our ideas about God against divine reality, and so propositions about God derived from scripture, tradition, or reason should not be treated as literally true but only as attempts to make sense of human experiences and ideas. At one extreme, theological anti-realism can seem akin to atheism. There is also a more orthodox tradition of mystical and 'negative' theology which emphasizes the gulf between the transcendence of God and the limited cognitive powers of mere humans, and draws the conclusion that it would be presumptuous to suppose any human formulation could grasp divine reality. One problem with this is that if human reason is too weak to make any true statements at all about the attributes of God, then it would seem that the statement that God exists does not amount to much. For that reason, many have continued to try to look beyond the seen to the unseen, hoping to succeed in the apparently impossible task of drawing back the veil of phenomena to discover how things really are.

Among those who believe they have succeeded in seeing behind the veil, there are conflicting accounts of what is to be found there – an impersonal cosmic machine, a chaos of matter in motion, a system governed by strict natural laws, or an omnipotent God acting in and through his creation. Which should we believe?

Chapter 3
Does God act in nature?

Supernatural signs and wonders have historically performed an important social function, marking out individuals, movements, or institutions as endowed with special God-given authority. The ability to perform miracles has been ascribed to revolutionaries, teachers, prophets, saints, and even to particular places and physical objects. The apparent power to resist the most irresistible of all forces – the forces of nature – has provided inspiration and hope to many communities facing persecution, poverty, or natural disasters.

Take, for example, the story of an early Christian martyr called Agatha. This beautiful and chaste young woman was a member of a group of persecuted Christians in 3rd-century Sicily. She rejected the amorous advances of a local Roman official, who punished her by banishing her to the local brothel. The legend has it that when Agatha refused to give up either her purity or her faith she was subjected to further tortures and punishments, which included having her breasts cut off with pincers. In Roman Catholic iconography, Agatha is sometimes depicted carrying her amputated breasts on a plate. Although her wounds were said to have been healed miraculously by a vision of St Peter, Agatha was condemned to further punishments, including being dragged across burning coals and broken glass. During this final punishment, the story goes, an earthquake was sent by God, which killed several Roman officials. Shortly afterwards Agatha herself died in prison.

The story of St Agatha, virgin and martyr, does not end there, however. After her death, Agatha was adopted by the people of Catania in Sicily as their protector and patron saint. According to local folklore, in the year after Agatha's death Mount Etna erupted, and when the martyr's veil was held up towards it, the volcanic lava was seen to change direction, leaving the city unharmed. The veil is reported to have protected the inhabitants of Catania from volcanic eruptions in the same miraculous way on several subsequent occasions. St Agatha's intercession is also credited by some believers with having prevented the plague from spreading to Catania in 1743. In these cases, the supernatural intervention of a particular saint was sought as protection against natural disasters which were themselves interpreted as acts of God. The supposed interactions between natural and supernatural agencies are not straightforward, but the message is clear: God cares for the people of Catania and, because of their association with St Agatha, will protect them.

The ability of God, either directly or through the intercession of specially chosen saints and prophets, to contravene the laws of nature in order to achieve his will is asserted by all the major religious traditions. God's various revelations of himself to Moses, to St Paul and the apostles, and through the angel Gabriel to Muhammad are themselves believed to be miraculous. The Bible records that Moses divided the Red Sea, that God sent plagues upon the Egyptians to punish them, and provided manna from heaven to feed his chosen people. The gospels assert that Jesus walked on water, healed the sick, brought the dead back to life, and was himself miraculously resurrected after dying on the cross. The Quran includes reports of miracles performed by Moses and Jesus, including an episode, not included in the Bible, when Jesus is said to have fashioned clay into the shape of a bird and miraculously breathed life into it to create a real bird.

5. St Agatha carrying her breasts on a plate, as depicted by the 17th-century painter Francisco de Zurbaran

Although there has been debate among Muslims about whether Muhammad himself performed any miracles, there is a reference in the Quran to the splitting of the moon, which was interpreted as miraculous confirmation of Muhammad's prophetic status.

Reports of miracles persist to this day. They frequently come in the form of miraculous cures of the kind sought by pilgrims to the shrine of the Blessed Virgin Mary at Lourdes in France, or by those who attend revivalist religious meetings presided over by charismatic preachers offering divine healing. From time to time there are reports of religious statues weeping blood or, as occurred in New Delhi in September 1995, drinking milk. When the story spread that statues of the Hindu deities Ganesh and Shiva had seemed to drink spoonfuls of milk, the phenomenon was soon being replicated in temples not only in India but all around the world, including in Britain, where some supermarkets experienced a sudden increase in demand for milk. In this case, as in most others, a rational and scientific explanation was soon offered – namely that the liquid was being drawn out of the spoon by capillary action (the same process that allows sponges and paper towels to absorb liquid), and was then simply running down the front of the statue. There was also a political explanation readily to hand. The ruling Congress Party in India claimed that the news of the alleged miracle was being spread by their Hindu nationalist opponents for electoral gain. The leader of one right-wing Hindu party, speaking in defence of the miracle, said: 'Scientists who dismiss it are talking nonsense. Most of them are atheists and communists.'

Signs, wonders, and miracles have a central place in religious traditions, whether as evidence of the special status of particular individuals, as proofs of the truth of particular doctrines, or as support for the broader secular and political aspirations of a movement. Although some believers welcome such things as apparent proofs of the reality and power of God, others are embarrassed by them. Reports of miracles seem, all too often, to be the results of such human weaknesses as wishful thinking, credulity, or even fraud, rather than anything supernatural. They can make religion seem superstitious and primitive. Believers as well as sceptics ask themselves whether stories of the miraculous and the supernatural are really credible in a scientific age. And, as we shall see in this chapter, the theological, philosophical, and moral questions raised about miracles are every bit as difficult to answer as the scientific ones.

The theologians' dilemma

Pity the poor theologians! They are faced with a seemingly impossible dilemma when it comes to making sense of divine action in the world. If they affirm that God does act through miraculous interventions in nature, then they must explain why God acts on these occasions but not on numerous others; why miracles are so poorly attested; and how they are supposed to be compatible with our scientific understanding of the universe. On the other hand, if they deny that God acts through special miraculous interventions, then they are left with a faith which seems to be little more than Deism – the belief that God created the universe but is no longer active within it. If God is real, should we not expect to be able to discern at least some special divine acts? The theologian seems to have to choose between a capricious, wonder-working, tinkering God and an absent, uninterested, undetectable one. Neither sounds like a suitable object for love and worship.

The job of the theologian is to try to articulate how God can act in and through nature while avoiding the two unattractive caricatures indicated above. Various distinctions have been employed to try to achieve this. One of these differentiates between the basic primary cause of all reality, which is God, and the secondary, natural causes employed to achieve divine purposes. Another distinguishes between God's 'general providence' – the way that nature and history have been set up to unfold according to the divine will – and rare acts of 'special providence', or miracles, in which God's power is more directly manifest. If those acts of special providence are restricted to a very small number – perhaps only those attested in scripture – or those associated with the lives of a very small number of important prophetic individuals – then God's interventions in the world might seem less capricious. Among both Christians and Muslims there are those who believe that the age in which God revealed himself in miracles and revelations has now passed.

As an example of the theologians' dilemma, consider the case of Lourdes. Millions of pilgrims flock to this town in the foothills of the Pyrenees each year – to the place where Bernadette, an illiterate and asthmatic peasant girl, saw an apparition of the Virgin Mary in 1858. Thousands claim to have been miraculously cured of physical ailments after drinking or bathing in the water of the spring uncovered by Bernadette. The Church is well aware of the potential natural explanations for such cures. Diagnoses can be mistaken. Diseases can go into remission unexpectedly. Psychosomatic cures are not uncommon. For these reasons there is an elaborate series of investigations that must be carried out before an alleged cure is declared miraculous. A panel of doctors appointed by the Lourdes International Medical Committee is required to study and confirm the reliability both of the original diagnosis and of the evidence that the cure at Lourdes was sudden, complete, and lasting. Those very few cases of cure for which the doctors are absolutely convinced that there is no possible natural or medical explanation are then put forward to the Church authorities, who have the power to declare the cure a miraculous 'sign of God'. Since 1858, the Church has declared only 67 miracles at Lourdes, out of the thousands of claimed cures. The most recent case added to the list was that of Anna Santaniello, who recovered suddenly from symptoms including severe asthma and acute arthritis during a visit to Lourdes in 1952. The Church had considered her case for 50 years before declaring it a miraculous cure.

6. A 19th-century image showing pilgrims to Lourdes praying at the place where Bernadette had her vision of the Virgin Mary. The grotto houses a statue of Mary; the crutches of those who have been cured hang in front of it.

The implementation of this cautious and highly selective process by which only a small proportion of claimed cures at Lourdes are declared miraculous is indicative of the need for the Church to retain credibility while also maintaining their traditional belief in special providence. Hasty claims of numerous spectacular miracles might give the impression of undue credulity or of an unacceptably meddlesome God. On the other hand, the hope that the supernatural can somehow break into the everyday lives of the faithful is a cornerstone of the Catholic faith, and the claim that it has done so lends support both to the doctrinal claims and to the worldly authority of the Catholic Church. The growth of Lourdes as a pilgrimage site in the 19th century was itself partly an expression of popular support for the Catholic Church in

France at a time when it was confronted by many secularist and rationalist detractors.

'As if God lived in the gaps?'

Protestant theologians have traditionally been somewhat more suspicious than Catholics about miracles (other than those recorded in the Bible). At the time of the Reformation, Protestants used the Catholic cult of the saints, especially of the Blessed Virgin Mary, and belief in the miraculous powers of holy relics, to portray the Church of Rome as superstitious and idolatrous. In more recent times, evangelical and Pentecostal forms of Protestant worship have involved wonders and miracles such as healings and speaking in tongues. However, there has been a continuous tradition of Protestant thought asserting that the age of miracles has passed and that divine activity is to be perceived in nature and history as a whole rather than in special interventions.

Two Protestant theologians illustrate this reinterpretation of the miraculous. The German thinker Friedrich Schleiermacher went so far as to redefine 'miracle' as 'merely the religious name for event', rather than as a happening which violated the laws of nature. In other words, a miracle was in the eye of the believer. In a series of lectures delivered in Boston in 1893, almost a century later, the Scottish evangelical theologian Henry Drummond, engaging the question of the proper Christian attitude to the theory of evolution, told his audience that a miracle was 'not *something quick*'. Rather, the whole, slow process of evolution was miraculous. Through that process God had produced not only the mountains and valleys, the sky and the sea, the flowers and the stars, but also 'that which of all other things in the universe commends itself, with increasing sureness as time goes on, to the reason and to the heart of Humanity – Love. Love is the final result of Evolution.' Drummond's point was that it was this product – love – rather than the particular process, natural or supernatural, which was the real miracle.

It was in this same lecture that Drummond introduced the idea of the 'God of the gaps'. He spoke of those 'reverent minds who ceaselessly scan the fields of Nature and the books of Science in search of gaps – gaps which they will fill up with God. As if God lived in the gaps?' God, he said, should be sought in human knowledge, not in human ignorance. He pointed out that if God is only to be found in special and occasional acts, then he must be supposed to be absent from the world the majority of the time. He asked whether the nobler conception was of a God present in everything or one present in occasional miracles. Drummond concluded that 'the idea of an immanent God, which is the God of Evolution, is infinitely grander than the occasional wonder-worker, who is the God of an old theology'.

The Medical Committee at Lourdes which finds signs of God only in those cases where a natural and scientific explanation is lacking, and proponents of 'Intelligent Design' who base their arguments for a designer on alleged inadequacies in evolutionary science, all seem guilty of advocating a God who resides only in gaps in current knowledge. As Drummond asked his audience, 'Where shall we be when these gaps are filled up?' On the other hand, what are we to make of Drummond's immanent God, and of the God of those contemporary theologians who see divine activity in the emergent complexity of the natural world? If God is in all natural processes equally, and even in all human actions and historical events equally too, then how can it be claimed that God is good, rather than bad or indifferent, or that God takes any special interest in human lives?

The whole history of modern science could be read as a parable designed to reinforce Drummond's warning against placing God in the gaps in current knowledge of the natural world. Isaac Newton, to take one very famous example, when confronted with questions such as why the planets in our solar system remained in their orbits rather than gradually slowing down and being drawn towards the sun, or why the distant stars were not all drawn towards each other by gravity, was prepared to hypothesize that God must intervene from time to time in order to keep the stars and planets in their proper positions. Newton's German rival and critic G. W. Leibniz attacked this hypothesis on theological grounds. Newton's God, Leibniz wrote in a letter of 1715, lacking sufficient foresight to make a properly functioning universe at the first attempt, apparently needed 'to *wind up* his watch from time to time' and 'to *clean* it now and then' and 'even to *mend* it, as a clockmaker mends his work; who must consequently be so much the more unskilful a workman, as he is oftener obliged to mend his work and to set it right'. Leibniz preferred to see God's involvement in the universe as one of perfect and complete foresight. As the theoretical and mathematical models of the solar system became even more accurate during the 18th and 19th centuries, there were increasing numbers who went even further. When asked by Napoleon about the place of God in his system, the French physicist Pierre Simon de Laplace allegedly replied that he 'had no need for that hypothesis'.

The histories of geology, natural history, and biology reveal a similar pattern of special divine actions (floods, volcanoes, and earthquakes; separate creations of the different species; intelligent design of each individual adaptation of creatures to their environments) gradually being pushed out of the scientific picture to be replaced by more gradual, uniform, and law-like natural processes. As we shall see in the next chapter, Charles Darwin's *On the Origin of Species*, published the year after Bernadette had her vision at Lourdes, made references to God, but only as the author of the laws of nature – those 'secondary causes' which seemed to be able to achieve the most wondrous results when impressed on matter, without any need for further interventions by the Creator.

The laws of nature

It was never the intention of the pioneers of modern science – men such as Isaac Newton, Robert Boyle, or René Descartes – to undermine religious belief. Far from it. They envisaged nature as an orderly system of mechanical interactions governed by mathematical laws. And they hoped that people would see in this new vision the strongest possible evidence of divine power and intelligence. In 1630 Descartes wrote to the Catholic theologian Marin Mersenne: 'God sets up mathematical laws in nature as a king sets up laws in his kingdom.' Most early modern scientists also took it for granted that God, who was responsible for determining the regular way in which nature would normally operate, was also quite capable of suspending or altering that normal course of nature whenever he so chose. Nonetheless, the method they adopted was one that has favoured a view of God as designer and lawgiver rather than as interventionist wonder-worker. The collaborative enterprise inaugurated by these scientific pioneers has proceeded on the assumption that natural phenomena are indeed governed by strict laws, which can be given precise mathematical expression. A further assumption made by many is that these laws will ultimately be reduced to a single unified theory. Does the success of science in explaining nature in terms of such laws amount to proof that God cannot act in nature?

Not necessarily. There are different ways of thinking about laws of nature. They need not be seen as entities or forces that somehow constrain all of reality. Instead, they can be interpreted in a more modest way as the best empirical generalizations we have so far arrived at to describe the behaviour of particular systems in particular contexts (often highly restricted experimental conditions that can be created only in laboratories). Nor are we obliged to believe that the laws of, say, physics are more 'fundamental' than the knowledge acquired through biology, sociology, or everyday experience. Although quantum theory provides exceedingly accurate empirical predictions when dealing with atomic and subatomic entities, it is not applicable to larger and more complex systems such as volcanoes, veils, or virgins, the behaviour of which can be more successfully explained by geology, materials science, and psychology, respectively. Furthermore, two of the most successful physical theories – general relativity and quantum mechanics – are both supposed to apply universally and yet are not compatible with each other. As the philosopher of science Nancy Cartwright has put it, what modern science seems to show is not that we live in a world governed by a single systematic set of natural laws that apply at all times and in all places, but rather that we live in a 'dappled world' in which pockets of order emerge, or can be made to emerge, using a patchwork of different scientific theories (from physics, to biology, to economics), none of which is applicable across all domains.

Another assumption behind the claim, made by some polemical atheists, that modern science has shown that miracles are impossible is the belief that the natural world is deterministic – in other words, that if we had perfect knowledge of the current state of the material world and of the laws that governed it, then in effect we would also have perfect knowledge of the future of the world (and that future would be as fixed and unalterable as the past). Again, these are not things that can be proved by experience or by science (not least because there is no prospect of our ever reaching the position of omniscience required in order to test the hypothesis). Belief in determinism rests on a range of related assumptions about such basic concepts as matter, causation, and laws of nature. It is, however, as professional philosophers have repeatedly and frequently proved, in the nature of such basic concepts that they rapidly start to crumble when subjected to attempts at clear and uncontroversial definition.

Quantum mechanics

In addition to the considerable philosophical perplexities involved in articulating, let alone defending, any kind of determinism, an important scientific challenge to the doctrine arose in the early 20th century in the form of quantum mechanics. Quantum theory resulted from physicists' attempts to understand the world of the very small – the behaviour of atomic and subatomic particles. Max Planck and Albert Einstein showed that light, then understood as an electromagnetic wave, also behaved as if it were made up of discrete particles, which came to be known as 'photons'. The implications of the theories later developed in the 1920s by quantum pioneers such as Erwin Schrödinger and Werner Heisenberg were wide-ranging, and their interpretation is still the subject of controversy. Einstein himself was unhappy with the probabilistic and indeterministic interpretations of quantum theory that came to predominate, saying that 'God does not play dice with the universe'. Some philosophers and physicists still share Einstein's unease. Having an instinctive preference for deterministic explanations, they hope to find a different interpretation of the laws of quantum physics.

The main reason, then, that quantum theory is controversial is that it seems to overturn many of the basic assumptions of classical Newtonian mechanics. It suggests that physics can no longer be reduced to a series of deterministic interactions between solid particles of matter. According to quantum theory, entities such as photons and electrons are simultaneously both particles and waves. Whether they seem to behave like one or the other depends on how the experimental apparatus interacts with them. Heisenberg's uncertainty principle further dictates that the momentum or the position of a quantum entity can be known, but never both. Finally, the observer has a key role in quantum theory, not just as a passive recipient of data, but as an active contributor to it. Quantum systems are governed by probabilistic 'wave functions' which do not take on a determinate value until they are observed. The act of observation is said to lead to the 'collapse of the wave function' and to resolve the system into one determinate state or position rather than another. Prior to observation, the system is held to be a 'cloud' consisting of all the possible observable states, each with a different probability assigned to it.

Even this brief and inexpert summary of some of the findings of quantum physics is hopefully enough to give a sense of how far we have come from the world of classical materialistic determinism. Quantum mechanics suggests that at the most basic level material reality is not deterministic (nor does it even seem to be 'material'). We are in a world of clouds, of wave functions, of probabilities – not the reassuringly picturable clockwork universe of the Enlightenment. Quantum theory also undermines the idea that the physical world exists objectively and independently of human observers, since it is the act of observation, or measurement, that collapses the wave function. The solid physical world of our everyday experience and of Newtonian physics in some sense comes into existence only by being measured.

Quantum physics is an absolutely central part of modern science, and the fact that the picture of physical reality that it offers is so strange and indeterministic has unsurprisingly proved of great interest to philosophical and religious thinkers. The prospect of a new and more holistic philosophy of nature in which the observer is integrally involved and in which determinism is denied is one that appeals to proponents of many different world views, from traditional religions to more modern 'New Age' ideologies. Attempts by theologians to make use of quantum physics as a more permanent source of 'gaps' in which God might be able to act have had a mixed reception. Such attempts do not help to answer the sceptic's question of why God would act on some occasions rather than others; nor do they satisfy those religious believers who hold that, as the author rather than the slave of the laws of nature, God can override or suspend them at will without needing to tinker with the states of quantum systems.

The first cause

But perhaps the fundamental laws of the physical universe themselves – rather than isolated suspensions, violations, or manipulations of those laws – provide the strongest evidence of divine purpose. This is to return to the simple idea suggested by many philosophers, theologians, and scientists through the ages that, although we might generally explain natural phenomena in terms of other secondary natural causes, we must, to avoid an endless regress, at some point posit a first cause, a 'prime mover', and that what we know of the world suggests that this prime mover is that same God whom many have encountered through sacred texts and religious experiences.

We cannot expect the natural sciences to help us with the question of a first cause. Science is unable to tell us why there is something rather than nothing. Cosmological theories can try to explain how the something that does exist works and how it is related to other cosmic somethings that have existed in the past, present, or future, or even in numerous parallel universes or extra dimensions. That is what is attempted by theories about big bangs and big crunches, about superstrings and membranes, and about quantum fluctuations and multiple universes. But physical science cannot go beyond that to explain why the things that we call matter-energy and laws of nature ever came to be. Here we have an unclosable gap in our scientific knowledge, and one which all theists agree is filled by God.

Atheists respond that even if we suppose the universe to have a creator or a designer, that does not answer the question of who created the creator or who designed the designer. This is true, but not very surprising. Every explanatory journey has a terminus. That terminus might be matter, or mystery, or metaphysical necessity. It might be a featureless first cause or it might be God. Wherever one decides to end the explanatory journey, there will always still be the possibility of asking 'Why?' or 'But what caused that?' The answer in all cases – whether religious or secular – is that something or other just is. A much more serious problem for the theist is how to close the large gap between positing a first cause for the universe and identifying that unknown cause with the personal God of Judaism, Christianity, Islam, or any other religious tradition.

Fine tuning

For those who see God in the arrangement of the laws of nature rather than in their occasional violation, it is notable that the universe seems to be 'fine tuned' for carbon-based life. If the physical constants of the universe had been very slightly different, then such life (including human life) would not have been possible. If the Big Bang had banged only slightly more vigorously, for example, matter would have been blown apart too fast for stars and planets to be formed. If the force of gravity had been even infinitesimally larger or smaller, then life-sustaining stars such as our sun could not have come into existence. Does this show that, to quote the physicist Fred Hoyle, 'a superintellect has monkeyed with physics' and that 'there are no blind forces worth speaking about in nature'? Some think that this fine tuning is indeed best explained by supposing that a creator with an interest in producing intelligent life designed our universe. Others are more persuaded by the idea that our universe is just one of countless universes in a 'multiverse' or a 'megaverse'. If that were the case, then at least a small proportion of those multiple universes would have the right conditions for producing life and, inevitably, we would find ourselves in one such universe.

What people on both sides of this argument agree about, but which should not be taken for granted, is that there is something here to be explained – whether by God or by multiverses. Both sides start with the premise that the values taken by the fundamental constants in our universe are surprising, improbable, and in need of explanation. But how do we know the probability of any given configuration of physical constants? Surely any specified combination of infinitely variable constants is equally, infinitely improbable? How, in any case, can we be confident that these constants are free to vary in the way these arguments assume they are, and are not simply fixed by nature or linked to each other in a way we do not understand? And should the actual existence of trillions of other universes, as opposed to their merely possible existence, really make us any less surprised about the existence and physical make-up of our own? As the character Philo put it in David Hume's *Dialogues Concerning Natural Religion* (1779),

> having found, in so many other subjects much more familiar, the imperfections and even contradictions of human reason, I never should expect any success from its feeble conjectures, in a subject so sublime, and so remote from the sphere of our observation.

Not seeing and yet believing

Hume was also the author of the most famous expression of rationalist scepticism about miracles. In a 1748 essay 'Of Miracles', Hume argued against miracles on the basis of the relative weakness of the evidence in favour of them. Since the laws of nature are, by definition, generalizations that conform as closely as possible to the universal experience of humanity, Hume said, then they are as empirically well grounded as any statement can be. However generous we wish to be about the strength of the evidence in favour of miracles – that is, the reports of supposed eye-witnesses to the events, such as those recorded in the scriptures and in lives of saints – that testimony will never be as strong as the evidence that supports the laws of nature. Which, Hume asked, would be the greater miracle – that the laws of nature had actually been overturned or that those attesting to the miracle (possibly even including yourself) were mistaken? A rational person, Hume concluded, would have to answer that the falsity of the testimony was the more likely option. In short, a rational person could not believe in miracles. To put this in terms of the different sources of knowledge discussed in Chapter 2, Hume's argument was that collective sense experience trumps testimony.

For those accepting the empiricist spirit of Hume's approach, even if not his conclusions, the evidence of one's own senses must indeed be the final court of appeal. No matter what your beliefs about physical science, the laws of nature, or the strength of the testimony of others to miracles, your own experience will override all of these. If you have never witnessed a miracle, that will probably be the most significant obstacle to your believing that such a thing can occur. If, on the other hand, you had witnessed with your own eyes St Agatha's wounds being instantaneously healed, or a flow of lava suddenly and inexplicably changing direction when a veil was held up to it, you would have to admit that you had seen something truly extraordinary, which, in spite of Hume, you might well consider a miracle.

Even then, however, there would be a gap between the observation that something had happened which was contrary to the normal course of nature, and the belief that you had witnessed a supernatural or divine event. A more scientific attitude would be to treat the event as an unexplained anomaly – like an experiment in the laboratory that does not produce the result predicted by your theory. Such anomalies might lead to new discoveries about how the natural world works, or they might remain recalcitrant and unexplained. They need not take on religious significance, however. It is the experience of remarkable and unexplained phenomena in a specifically religious context that turns an anomaly into a miracle.

One religious response to the rationalist's demand for better evidence for miracles is to suggest that religious truths are to be accepted not on the basis of empirical evidence but through faith. The importance of faith is strongly emphasized in the New Testament – most famously in the story of the apostle Thomas, who says that he will not believe Jesus has risen from the dead until he sees him in the flesh with the marks of the nails in his hands and the wound in his side. Thomas then encounters the

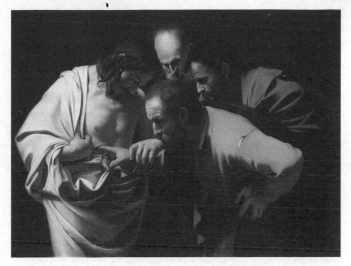

7. Caravaggio's *The Incredulity of St Thomas* (1602–3)

risen Jesus, and believes. Jesus says to Thomas: 'Because you
have seen me, you have believed; blessed are those who have not
seen and yet have believed.' In his anti-Christian polemic *The
Age of Reason* (1794), Thomas Paine remarked that if Thomas
could refuse to believe in the resurrection until he had 'ocular
and manual demonstration', then so could he, 'and the reason is
equally as good for me, and for every other person, as for Thomas'.
More recently, Richard Dawkins has described Thomas as the
'only really admirable member of the twelve apostles', because of
his scientific demand for empirical evidence.

Divine inaction

The rebellious and sceptical Ivan, one of the brothers in
Dostoyevsky's novel *The Brothers Karamazov* (1880), like
doubting Thomas, demands evidence. He is disgusted by the
human cruelty and suffering that he sees all around, and does

not accept that the promise of a future life in which all will be well is a satisfactory recompense. 'I want to see with my own eyes the lion lie down with the lamb and the murdered man rise up and embrace his murderer', Ivan tells his brother. 'I want to be there when everyone suddenly finds out what it has all been for.' But until that happens, Ivan cannot believe that the suffering of innocent children at the hands of torturers and abusers can ever be made up for by any future heavenly rewards. If that is the price of eternal truth and of admission to heaven, Ivan says, then the price is too high, and 'I hasten to return my ticket of admission.'

Ivan's rejection of Christianity is one that has been echoed by countless other critics of religion. If God exists and has the power to intervene in nature, and on occasion apparently uses that power, they ask, why does God fail to intervene in so many other cases of horrific injustice, cruelty, and suffering? Why, for example, did God allow Agatha to be tortured, abused, and mutilated before miraculously healing her through a vision of St Peter? Why would God allow some to be killed by volcanic eruptions and plagues, while bestowing special protection on the inhabitants of Catania? Why, in any case, does God need to use the powers of an object such as St Agatha's veil to achieve this protection, rather than acting directly to prevent the eruption or the disease in the first place? More generally, why is one person miraculously cured while another of equal faith and virtue suffers and dies? We might say that God moves in a mysterious way – which certainly seems to have been the case if we are to believe the many religious tales of wonders and miracles through the ages – but is that a good enough response? If God created us and our moral sense, then why do God's own ways of acting in the world seem to us not to meet our own standards of what is just and good?

These are among the most difficult questions with which religious believers have to grapple. As Henry Drummond put it, 'If God appears periodically, He disappears periodically. If He comes upon the scene at special crises, He is absent from the scene in the intervals.' Science and philosophy certainly do not require us to believe in determinism or to deny the possibility of miracles. However, the theologians' dilemma will not go away: divine inaction is just as hard to explain as divine action.

Chapter 4
Darwin and evolution

When the English naturalist Charles Darwin died at his Kent home in April 1882 at the age of 73, he was already a celebrity. Not only in Britain but around the world he was famed as the author of the theory of evolution that had transformed science and become the defining philosophy of the age. The news of his death was greeted by a campaign in the press for a funeral at Westminster Abbey. Despite lingering doubts about Darwin's religious beliefs, it was soon agreed that no other tribute would be adequate. The great and the good would gather to mark the astonishing theoretical achievements, the patience and industry of decades of research, and the dignity and modesty of this unassuming English gentleman. At the funeral, the Reverend Frederic Farrar's sermon compared Darwin's scientific genius with that of his countryman, Isaac Newton, next to whose memorial in the abbey Darwin's own final resting place would be. Farrar also explained that Darwin's theory of evolution was quite consistent with an elevated sense of the actions of the Creator in the natural world. The funeral symbolized the acceptance by the Anglican establishment of Darwin and of evolution, just over 20 years after the publication of *On the Origin of Species* in 1859.

It was a somewhat suspicious and hesitant kind of acceptance, though. Not everyone in the Church of England, nor in society at large, was happy to 'go the whole orang' – the geologist Charles Lyell's phrase for accepting that evolution applied to humans too. Indeed, it has always been human evolution in particular, rather than the evolution of bacteria, beetles, barnacles, or bats, that has really captured the imagination and unsettled the beliefs of the wider public. Religious ideas about the elevated place of humanity in the creation, and especially about the soul and morality, were the ones most directly challenged by the evolutionary science that Darwin's career helped to establish as a new orthodoxy. Among those who have resisted Darwinism for religious reasons over the last century and a half, some have done so on the grounds of its conflict with a literal interpretation of scripture. For many others, however, their resistance has been to the theory of evolution's apparent incompatibility with belief in free will, moral responsibility, and a rational and immortal human soul.

In this chapter and the next, we will explore these and other reasons why the theory of evolution has been considered so dangerous, starting in this chapter with Darwin's religious views, the reception of his theory, and its theological implications, before moving on in Chapter 5 to the modern American controversy about teaching evolution in schools. The figure of Charles Darwin himself continues to haunt these discussions. His image adorns not only the covers of countless books on the subject of evolution but also even the British ten pound note. The most frequently used pictures of Darwin are those from his old age in which his white beard and portentous expression conjure up images of biblical prophets, perhaps even of God. The theory of evolution by natural selection has become identified with this single iconic historical individual. Darwin's own scientific and religious views are often discussed and sometimes misrepresented in polemical works about evolution and religion. It is important therefore to have a grasp of what this revolutionary scientific thinker really thought and why.

8. A photographic portrait of Charles Darwin made by Lock and Whitfield in 1878

Darwin's religious odyssey

In his early 20s, Darwin was looking forward to a career in the Church of England. He had embarked on medical training in Edinburgh a few years earlier but had found the lectures boring and the demonstrations of surgery disgusting. Now his father sent him off to Christ's College, Cambridge, where young Charles signed up to the Thirty-Nine Articles of the Church of England and set about studying mathematics and theology with a view to entering holy orders after graduation. But Darwin found that theology appealed about as much as surgery. His real passion at this time was for beetle-hunting rather than Bible-reading, and he had an early triumph when one of the specimens he had identified appeared in print in an instalment of *Illustrations of British Entomology*. In 1831 this enthusiastic young amateur naturalist was invited to join the *HMS Beagle* as a companion to the ship's captain, Robert Fitzroy, and to undertake collections and observations on matters of natural-historical interest. Perhaps he was not, after all, destined to become the Reverend Charles Darwin.

The voyage of the *Beagle* lasted from 1831 to 1836. The primary purpose of the expedition was to complete the British Admiralty's survey of the coast of South America, but its five-year itinerary also took in Australia, New Zealand, and South Africa. Darwin's observations of rock formations, plants, animals, and indigenous peoples were incidental to the purpose of the expedition but absolutely central to his own intellectual development. On board the *Beagle*, Darwin's religious views started to evolve too. He had no doubt that the natural world was the work of God. In his notebook he recorded his impressions of the South American jungle: 'Twiners entwining twiners – tresses like hair – beautiful lepidoptera – Silence – hosannah.' To Darwin, these jungles were 'temples filled with the varied productions of the God of Nature', in which no-one could stand without 'feeling that there is more in man than the mere breath of his body'. He even admired the civilizing effects of the work of Christian missionaries too, observing that 'so excellent is the Christian faith, that the outward conduct of the believers is said most decidedly to have been improved by its doctrines'.

Back in England, however, after the voyage, Darwin would start to have doubts. His grandfather, father, and elder brother had all rejected Christianity, adopting either Deism or outright freethinking unbelief. He seemed to be heading in a similar direction. His reasons were many. His travels had revealed to him at first hand the great variety of religious beliefs and practices around the world. All these different religions claimed to have a special revelation from God, but they could not all be right. Then there was his moral revulsion at the Christian doctrine that while the faithful would be saved, unbelievers and heathens, along with unrepentant sinners, would be consigned to an eternity of damnation. Darwin thought this was a 'damnable doctrine' and could not see how anyone could wish it to be true. This objection hit him with particular force after the death of his unbelieving father in 1848.

There were two ways in which Darwin's re-reading of the book of nature also gave him reasons to re-think his religion. He and others before him had seen in the adaptation of plants and animals to their environments evidence of the power and wisdom of God. But Darwin now thought he saw something else. Hard though it was for him to believe it himself – the human eye could still give him a shudder of incredulity – he came to think that all these adaptations came about by natural processes. Variation and natural selection could counterfeit intelligent design. Secondly, along with the silent beauty of the jungle he had also observed all sorts of cruelty and violence in nature, which he could not believe a benevolent and omnipotent God could have willed. Why, for example, would God have created the ichneumon wasp? The ichneumon lays its eggs inside a caterpillar, with the effect that when the larvae hatch they eat their host alive. Why would God create cuckoos which eject their foster siblings from the nest? Why make ants that enslave other species of ant? Why give queen bees the instinct of murderous hatred towards their daughters? 'What a book a Devil's chaplain might write', Darwin exclaimed, 'on the clumsy, wasteful, blundering low & horridly cruel works of nature!'

9. An ichneumon wasp injecting its eggs into the caterpillar that will play host to the wasp larvae and, in due course, provide their first meal

Darwin never became an atheist. At the time he wrote *On the Origin of Species* he was still a theist, although not a Christian. By the end of his life he preferred to adopt the label 'agnostic', which had been coined by his friend Thomas Huxley in 1869. Darwin, for the most part, kept his religious doubts to himself. He had many reasons to do so, not least his desire for a quiet life and social respectability. The most important reason, though, was his wife Emma. In the early years of their marriage, Emma, a pious evangelical Christian, wrote a letter to Charles of her fears about his loss of faith in Christianity and the consequences for his salvation. She could not bear the thought that his doubts would mean they were not reunited after death in heaven. The death of their beloved young daughter Annie in 1851 brought home again the need for the consolation of an afterlife. The difference between Charles and Emma on this question was a painful one. Among Darwin's papers after his death, Emma found the letter she had written to him on the subject 40 years earlier. On it her husband had added a short note of his own: 'When I am dead, know that many times, I have kissed and cryed over this.'

The theory of evolution by natural selection

The observations made by Darwin during his *Beagle* voyage proved crucial to his later theoretical speculations. As with all scientific observations, these only made sense with reference to existing theoretical frameworks, in this case to William Paley's natural theology and Charles Lyell's geology. On his return to England, reading a work of political economy by the Reverend Thomas Malthus would provide Darwin with a further and critically important idea, which would become the linchpin of his theory.

Like all Cambridge students at the time, Darwin was well versed in the works of William Paley. An Anglican clergyman, philosopher, and theologian, Paley was one of the most popular religious writers of the 18th and 19th centuries. His 1802 book *Natural Theology, or Evidence of the Existence and Attributes of the Deity, Collected from the Appearances of Nature* compared plants and animals to a pocket watch. Any structure with many intricately crafted parts working together to achieve a specified end – telling the time in the one case, gathering pollen, flying, or seeing, in the other – must have had a designer. Just as a watch has a human watchmaker, Paley reasoned, to the satisfaction of the young Darwin and tens of thousands of other readers, so the works of nature – its flowers and its bees, its birds' wings and its human eyes – must have had a supremely powerful and intelligent designer, namely God. Unlike Thomas Paine and the Deists, who took this argument as the main basis for their religion, Paley thought that this kind of natural theology was of use largely as a supplementary argument confirming what was already known from the Bible, and from the inner voice of one's conscience. What Darwin specifically took from Paley was the tendency to find everywhere in nature extraordinary evidence of design, of contrivance, of adaptation.

A second key component of Darwin's world view was provided by a book he read during the *Beagle* voyage, Sir Charles Lyell's *Principles of Geology*, published in three volumes between 1830 and 1833. Lyell's book argued that the history of the earth was one of gradual changes operating over long periods of time rather than one of regular violent catastrophes. His was a reformist rather than a revolutionary view of geology – time was to replace violence as the principal agent of change. Darwin came to see geological phenomena through Lyell's eyes. He witnessed an earthquake, for example, in Chile in 1835. After the quake he noticed that the shoreline had risen slightly. He also observed similar elevated beaches at much higher levels up in the Andes. If geological change could be explained by such gradual modifications over time, perhaps biological change could too. Darwin later confessed, 'I always feel as if my books came half out of Lyell's brains.'

When Darwin got back to England and started to try to make sense of the numerous specimens of plants and animals he had collected during the voyage, he began to focus on the 'species question'. This was the 'mystery of mysteries' for those seeking a naturalistic explanation of the origins of the different forms of life. In the 1830s, Darwin was confronted with two alternative explanations which were both equally unpalatable to him. Either each species had been created at a particular time and place by God, as most other naturalists believed, or else all life had started, perhaps spontaneously, in a simple form and had gradually climbed the ladder of life in the direction of greater complexity and perfection. The first option was unattractive because it posited a whole series of miraculous interventions by God in the history of life. What Darwin wanted to find was an explanation in terms of natural laws. The second option, the French naturalist Jean-Baptiste Lamarck's theory of 'transmutation', developed in his *Philosophie Zoologique* (1809), involved too many unacceptable theoretical assumptions for Darwin, such as the idea that life was continuously being spontaneously generated and starting its ascent up the ladder of life, that all life was climbing in the same direction up this single ladder, and that a creature's own voluntary efforts could alter its physical structure. Lamarck's theory was also widely believed to be connected to religiously unacceptable ideas of materialism and determinism – in other words, to the view that all phenomena, both mental and physical, could ultimately be explained in terms of causal interactions between particles of matter.

The animal life of the Galapagos islands – its finches and giant tortoises, its iguanas and mocking birds – was later to provide one of the keys to unlocking the 'mystery of mysteries'. During his five weeks on the island in 1835, Darwin became aware that these creatures differed in form from one island to the next, and also between the islands and the South American mainland. Subsequently, back in England, Darwin started to see these differences as useful evidence for evolution. At the time, he did not take great care to mark which finches had been collected from which island. And in the case of the giant tortoises, he even ate some of the evidence, recording in his diary: 'Eating tortoise meat. By the way delicious in soup.'

The Galapagos finches have become a popular example with which to explain Darwin's theory since they nicely illustrate the dilemma he faced as he thought about the history of life in the 1830s. Each island had its own species of finch, with differences in the sizes and shapes of their beaks. Did this require Darwin to believe that there had been a separate act of creation by God on each island, and another one on the mainland too? This seemed scientifically and theologically inelegant, to say the least. A unidirectional transmutationist model would not work either, since there was no obvious way to arrange these different species in a single line with one developing into the other. From the late 1830s, Darwin filled his notebooks with arguments and

10. A giant Galapagos tortoise of the kind Darwin enjoyed eating during his visit to the islands in 1835

counter-arguments trying to solve these sorts of problems. He thought about the way that breeders of pigeons selected particular individuals among each generation when trying to produce unusual new varieties. The analogy with artificial selection would be central to his argument. Even more central, though, was an idea he took from *An Essay on the Principle of Population* (1798) by Thomas Malthus.

Darwin read Malthus's *Essay* in 1838 and saw how it could be applied to the species question. Malthus's concern was with human populations. He believed that these had a natural tendency

1. Geospiza magnirostris.
2. Geospiza fortis.
3. Geospiza parvula.
4. Certhidea olivasea.

11. An illustration from Darwin's *Journal of Researches into the Natural History and Geology of the Countries Visited During the Voyage of H.M.S. Beagle* (1845), showing a selection of the different species of finch collected during the voyage

to increase at an exponential rate from one generation to the next (1, 2, 4, 8 ...), while the amount of food that a society could produce increased only arithmetically (1, 2, 3, 4 ...). This led, in each generation, to a struggle for resources. The strong would survive but the weak would perish. Looking at the entangled creepers of the South American jungle, the parasitic and murderous instincts of insects, and even at the plants and weeds in his own back garden, Darwin could see something similar going on – a competition for resources which those creatures with even a slight advantage over their competitors would win. This struggle for existence and the resulting 'survival of the fittest', as the evolutionary philosopher Herbert Spencer would call it, became the central idea of Darwin's theory. Alfred Russel Wallace, who came up with the idea of natural selection in the 1850s, 20 years later than Darwin but before Darwin had published his theory, also gave credit to Malthus as a source of inspiration.

Darwin now had his solution. The adaptation of organisms to their environment, and the origins of separate species, should be explained not in terms of the creative acts of Paley's designer, but by geographical distribution, random heritable variation, competition for resources, and the survival of the fittest over vast aeons of time. Natural selection could come in many different guises – as a disease, a predator, a drought, a shortage of your favourite food, a sudden change in the weather – but those individuals in each generation who happened by good luck to be the best equipped to cope with these natural assaults would flourish and leave offspring, while the less well adapted would perish without issue. Repeat that process for hundreds of millions of years and the whole panoply of species now observed could evolve from the simplest forms of life.

So, according to this theory, the species of Galapagos finches were not separately created, nor were they on the successive rungs of a single ladder of life; instead, they were at the ends of different branches of a huge family tree – the tree of life. The differences in the kinds of food that had been available on the different islands – seeds, insects, or cactuses – meant that different sizes and shapes of beak would have bestowed a greater advantage in the struggle for existence depending on geographical location. These species had diverged from a common ancestor species, originally blown across from the mainland. Nature had then acted like the pigeon-fancier, selecting those individuals with the desired characteristics, and allowing them to breed.

When, in 1858, Darwin received a letter from Wallace outlining a theory virtually identical to his, he was spurred into a more rapid publication of his ideas than he had planned. At a hurriedly arranged meeting of the Linnaean Society, an announcement was made of Darwin's and Wallace's theories. The following year saw

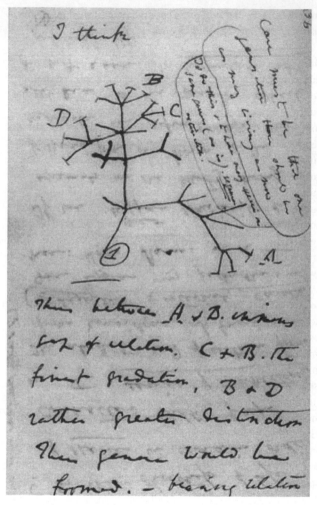

12. One of Darwin's first sketches, in his notebooks of the late 1830s, of his idea of a branching tree of life connecting all organisms through a shared ancestry

the publication by John Murray of Albemarle Street, London, of *On the Origin of Species by Means of Natural Selection, or The Preservation of Favoured Races in the Struggle for Life*. The author's credentials were prominently displayed on the title page: 'Charles Darwin, M.A., Fellow of the Royal, Geological, Linnaean, etc., Societies; Author of *Journal of Researches During H.M.S. Beagle's Voyage Round the World*'. Hopefully this impressive potted curriculum vitae would make the book's revolutionary contents more palatable to its Victorian readers.

'Our unsuspected cousinship with the mushrooms'

Those first readers of *On the Origin of Species* were presented with a view of nature in which God had been pushed to the margins rather than banished completely. God was no longer needed to create each individual species but Darwin, whether for the sake of convention or out of his own remaining religious convictions, presented his argument as favouring a kind of theistic evolution. On opening their copy of the book in 1859, the first words that a reader would have come across were two theological epigraphs – one a quotation from the Anglican divine and polymath, William Whewell, the other from Francis Bacon, one of the leading lights of the scientific revolution of the 17th century. Whewell stated that in the material world 'events are brought about not by insulated interpositions of Divine power, exerted in each particular case, but by the establishment of general laws'. According to Bacon, one could never have too much knowledge of either the book of God's word or the book of God's works, divinity or philosophy, 'rather let men endeavour an endless progress or proficience in both'.

When it came to the concluding section of the book, Darwin reiterated Whewell's view that God acted in a law-like rather than a miraculous fashion. 'To my mind,' Darwin wrote, it accords better with what we know of the laws impressed on matter by the Creator, that the production and extinction of the past and present inhabitants of the world should have been due to secondary causes … When I view all beings not as special creations, but as the lineal descendants of some few beings which lived long before the first bed of the Silurian system was deposited, they seem to me to become ennobled.

In the famous closing sentences of the book, Darwin marvelled that from 'the war of nature, from famine and death', the highest forms of life had been produced. He concluded:

There is grandeur in this view of life, with its several powers, having been originally breathed into a few forms or into one; and that, whilst this planet has gone cycling on according to the fixed law of gravity, from so simple a beginning endless forms most beautiful and most wonderful have been, and are being, evolved.

From the second edition onwards, in case there was any doubt about his meaning, he changed the phrase 'breathed into a few forms or into one' to 'breathed by the Creator into a few forms or into one'.

There were some within the Christian churches who were persuaded by Darwin's new natural theology. There was indeed greater grandeur and nobility, they agreed, as well as more simplicity and order, in a world where God had created through a law-like process of evolution, rather than one in which God periodically intervened to top up the planet's flora and fauna after particularly destructive catastrophes. We have already seen in Chapter 3 that Henry Drummond was one such individual. The historian, Christian socialist, and novelist Charles Kingsley was another. His famous children's story *The Water Babies*, published in 1863, included an allusion to his approval for Darwin's new theory. The little boy Tom approaches 'Mother Carey', a personification of nature, and says 'I heard, ma'am, that you were always making new beasts out of old.' Mother Carey replies 'So people fancy. But I am not going to trouble myself to make things, my little dear. I sit here and make them make themselves.' A future Archbishop of Canterbury, Frederick Temple, was another Anglican who supported the idea that God might have created through variation and natural selection rather than by a succession of miracles. On the other side of the Atlantic also there were individuals, such as the Harvard botanist and Presbyterian Asa Gray, who were persuaded to adopt a theistic version of Darwinian evolution.

But there were instances of conflict too, most famously in the form of a dramatic confrontation at the British Association for the Advancement of Science in Oxford in 1860. Darwin himself was not present at the occasion, but his theory was discussed in a paper applying Darwinian ideas to the question of intellectual and social progress. The general issue of Darwinism was then opened up to the floor for further debate. The first speaker was the Bishop of Oxford, Samuel Wilberforce. He spoke at some length about Darwin's theory. We do not have a record of exactly what he said, but we can make an educated guess based on his review of *On the Origin of Species* which appeared in the conservative *Quarterly Review*. In that review, Wilberforce noted that the conclusion implied by Darwin's book, namely that 'mosses, grasses, turnips, oaks, worms, and flies, mites and elephants, infusoria and whales, tadpoles of today and venerable saurians, truffles and men, are all equally the lineal descendants of the same aboriginal common ancestor' was certainly a surprising one, but one which he would have to admit if the scientific reasoning were sound. He was not going to object, he wrote, to Darwin's inference of 'our unsuspected cousinship with the mushrooms' on biblical grounds, since it was most unwise to try to judge the truth of scientific theories with reference to revelation. However, drawing heavily on the work of the country's leading anatomist, Richard Owen, Wilberforce found plenty of scientific objections to the theory, focusing especially on the lack of fossil evidence of transitional forms, and on the fact that however many varieties of pigeons and dogs may have been produced under domestication, pigeons had always remained pigeons and dogs always dogs. There had been no hint of a new species.

Although he did not base his objections on a literal reading of the Bible, Wilberforce's resistance to evolution, like that of many religious believers since his day, did derive from a commitment to a biblically inspired world view in which human beings were separate from and superior to the rest of the animal world. The Christian teaching that God took on human form in the person of Jesus Christ also gave that human form a particularly special significance. To claim that man was nothing more than an 'improved ape' rather than 'Creation's crown and perfection' was, Wilberforce pointed out, therefore demeaning to God as well as to humanity. At the Oxford meeting, at the end of his remarks, Wilberforce is reported to have turned to one of Darwin's staunchest advocates, Thomas Huxley, who was present among the throng of almost a thousand people, and asked him whether he was descended from an ape on the side of his grandmother or his grandfather. It was intended as a joke, but Huxley was apparently white with anger as he whispered to his neighbour, 'The Lord hath delivered him into mine hands.' Huxley rose and replied severely that he would rather be descended from an ape than from a man who used his intellect and influence to introduce ridicule into a grave scientific discussion. As the temperature in the packed auditorium rose, and at least one woman fainted in the excitement, Darwin's old companion from *HMS Beagle*, Captain Fitzroy, stood up holding a Bible aloft with both hands and denounced Darwin's theory. Another of Darwin's inner circle, the botanist Joseph Hooker, then weighed in with what was, on Hooker's own account, a decisive intervention on the side of Darwinism.

It is a colourful story, and one that has become part of Darwinian folklore. In 1860, Wilberforce, Huxley, and Hooker all thought

13. Cartoons from *Vanity Fair* depicting Professor Thomas Huxley and Bishop Samuel Wilberforce, whose encounter in Oxford in 1860 became legendary

that they had won the day. But by the time the tale came into wider circulation a couple of decades later, Huxley and Hooker, who had long been pressing for the autonomy of science from the Church, had risen to positions of much greater influence. The ascendancy of the professionalizing agnostics within the British scientific establishment was witnessed by the fact that both Hooker and Huxley were chosen to serve as Presidents of the Royal Society. The Huxley-Wilberforce story was then used retrospectively, as a piece of victors' history, to suggest a clearer triumph for scientific naturalism over Anglican conservatism than had really been achieved in Oxford in 1860. It suited the new elite to be able to tell the story in a way that seemed to foreshadow and legitimize their own rise to power, while simultaneously depoliticizing the issue. The 1860 confrontation between Samuel Wilberforce and Richard Owen, on the one hand, and the young Darwinians, on the other, had resulted from a struggle for dominance within the institutions of British science and education – a conflict between competing social interests as well as between competing interpretations of the scientific evidence for evolution. The later recasting of the Huxley-Wilberforce debate as one more instance of a simple and timeless conflict between 'science' and 'religion' helped to suggest that the agnostics' rise to power was the result of an inexorable historical process rather than a deliberate political campaign.

Evolution and theology

Wilberforce's review of *On the Origin of Species* identified the theological issues which would play out repeatedly among Christians, Jews, Muslims, and others as they considered the implications of evolution for their religious beliefs in the 19th century and afterwards. Some of these were not new. Discoveries in astronomy and geology had already given theologians plenty of opportunity to discuss the relative authority of science and scripture in determining natural knowledge. Darwin's view of nature drew particular attention to suffering, violence, and death. But people hardly needed Darwin to tell them that these were features of the natural world in general and of human life in particular. Again, theologians were already aware of the problem of evil, and had various responses to it. One common response to human evil was to explain that God must allow his creatures free will, which could be turned to either good or evil ends. Bishop Wilberforce's response to Darwin's remarks on imperfections in nature, and on the apparent cruelty of such creatures as the ichneumon wasp, was to refer to the Christian idea of the Fall. On this view, when Adam and Eve, the crowns and rulers of creation, were expelled from the Garden of Eden for their disobedience, it was not just they and their human descendants who fell from grace into a disordered state; it was the whole of nature. As Wilberforce put it, the 'strange forms of imperfection and suffering amongst the works of God' were the ongoing expression of 'the strong shudder which ran through all this world when its head and ruler fell'.

What was theologically new and troubling was the destruction of the boundary securely separating humanity from the 'brute creation' (and, to a lesser but significant extent, the destruction of the boundaries separating kinds of plants and animals from each other). The publication of Darwin's theories about human evolution in *The Descent of Man* (1871) and *The Expression of the Emotions in Man and Animals* (1872) provided further material for discussions about the relationship between humanity and the other animals. In these works Darwin speculated, as he had not dared to in 1859, on how even the most elevated of human faculties – the emotions, the moral sense, and religious feelings – might have evolved by natural means (including the 'Lamarckian' process of the inheritance of acquired characteristics, which Darwin always maintained operated alongside his own favoured mechanism of natural selection).

By the end of the 19th century, there was no serious scientific opposition to the basic evolutionary tenets of descent with modification and the common ancestry of all forms of life. There was considerable dispute about the explanatory sufficiency of the mechanism identified by Darwin and Wallace as the main driving force of evolution, namely natural selection acting on random variations. Lamarckian mechanisms of various forms were still discussed, and the process of heredity was a matter of dispute. From 1900 onwards, there were debates between those who used the work of Gregor Mendel to argue that characteristics were inherited in all-or-nothing units of the kind that came to be known as 'genes', and those who believed that inheritance was a question of an infinitely gradated 'blending' of traits. Only during the 1930s and 1940s did the modern evolutionary framework of neo-Darwinism, with which we are now familiar, take shape. That framework combined Mendelian genetics with the theory of natural selection, and finally rejected evolutionary theories that

THE
LONDON SKETCH BOOK.

PROF. DARWIN.

This is the ape of form.
Love's Labor Lost, act 5, scene 2.

Some four or five descents since.
All's Well that Ends Well, act 3, sc. 7.

14. One of many 19th-century images which satirized Darwin's theory of human evolution by depicting him as an ape

appealed either to the inheritance of acquired characteristics or to some innate life-force driving evolution from within.

Throughout these developments, theologians continued to make various uses of evolutionary ideas. The early 20th century saw a flourishing of ideas about creative evolution and guided evolution that appealed to religious thinkers. Since then, the triumph of neo-Darwinism has posed different theological problems. Within each faith tradition, there have been those who embrace evolution but also those who reject it – each has its own evolutionists, its own creationists, and many others in between.

For Jews, the theory of evolution not only raises questions about biblical interpretation and about human nature but also has connotations of Nazism and the Holocaust. Ideas about the 'survival of the fittest' were used by Nazis to try to justify their racist and eugenic ideology. Their regime was responsible for the murder of millions of Jews and others of supposedly 'inferior' races during the Second World War. The theory of evolution by natural selection has been used to bolster all sorts of different ideologies, including socialism, liberalism, and anarchism. Recent historical research has even shown how evolutionary ideas were used in the construction and defence of Zionism. While the idea of evolution has proved to be politically very malleable, it is generally accepted that in itself the scientific theory does not lead to any of these positions. Ideas of evolution will surely nonetheless continue to carry a menacing undertone given the anti-Semitic uses to which they have been put in the past. It has been pointed out that two biologists who were prominent in resisting more deterministic evolutionary theories of mind and society in the later 20th century, namely Stephen Jay Gould and Richard Lewontin, were both Jewish (although they both had scientific and political reasons for resisting such theories too).

Since the 19th century, the Roman Catholic Church has gradually developed an official line accepting that the human species has physically evolved in the way described by science, but which states that each individual human soul is created in the image of God and cannot be explained merely as the product of materialistic evolution. There have been Roman Catholics on and slightly beyond the fringes of orthodoxy who have spoken in favour of evolution, such as the 19th-century anatomist St George Mivart, who tried to persuade the Church of the plausibility of theistic evolution, and the Jesuit palaeontologist Pierre Teilhard de Chardin, whose popular mid-20th-century books interpreted evolution as a divinely guided cosmic process with human moral and spiritual awareness as its goal. Pope Benedict XVI, speaking at his inaugural mass in 2005, struck a cautionary note on the subject. 'We are not,' he said, 'some casual and meaningless product of evolution. Each of us is the result of a thought of God. Each of us is willed, each of us is loved, each of us is necessary.' The Roman Catholic Church has not generally been supportive of the anti-Darwinian 'Intelligent Design' movement, however. The Pope's warnings are not against evolution as science but against adopting the idea of evolution as an overarching view that deprives the world of meaning and purpose. It seems that the Catholic Church remains ambivalent towards evolution. One of the leading advocates of 'Intelligent Design', Michael Behe, and one of its most accomplished scientific critics, Kenneth Miller, are both Roman Catholics.

In recent decades, the most prominent religious opponents of evolution have come from within two particular traditions – Protestantism and Islam. The varieties of creationism that have emerged in these traditions in the 20th and 21st centuries are remote from the theological and scientific discussions about Darwinism that took place in the late 19th century. In order to understand the 20th-century rise of scientific creationism, we need now to turn our attention to the history and politics of the United States of America.

Chapter 5
Creationism and Intelligent Design

E. coli is the poster-bug for 'Intelligent Design'. It propels itself with an ingenious rotating tail or 'flagellum' – a sort of bacterial outboard motor. With its many connected parts working together towards the specified end of locomotion, this flagellum fulfils the criteria for design set out by William Paley in 1802. But surely the triumph of the modern theory of evolution has made it impossible to prefer Paley's theological explanation of such adaptations to Darwin's naturalistic one? Apparently not for everyone.

Since the early 1990s, supporters of the movement promoting 'Intelligent Design' or 'ID' in the United States have been mounting a challenge to the neo-Darwinian theory that all forms of life have evolved through the processes of genetic variation, heredity, and natural selection. Devotees of ID, including the lawyer Philip Johnson, the mathematician, philosopher, and theologian William Dembski, and the biochemist Michael Behe, say that it represents a serious scientific challenge to evolution. They think that certain aspects of the natural world, such as the bacterial flagellum, are too complex and too unlikely to have been produced by processes of genetic mutation and natural selection. And they use detailed calculations, based on debatable mathematical assumptions about information and probability, to quantify that unlikeliness and to justify their incredulity. Michael Behe focuses especially on complex chains of chemical processes within cells such as the series of reactions involved in the clotting of blood in mammals, known as the 'blood clotting cascade'. He is, if you like, Paley with a doctorate in biochemistry. The most plausible explanation of the 'irreducible complexity' of the flagellum, the blood clotting cascade, and many other phenomena which rely on complicated interactions between multiple components, Behe believes, is that they were produced by an intelligent designer (whom he and most of his readers suppose to be God).

The American Association for the Advancement of Science has stated that ID is characterized by 'significant conceptual flaws in its formulation, a lack of credible scientific evidence, and misrepresentations of scientific facts' and that its central concept is 'in fact religious, not scientific'. In a landmark case in Pennsylvania in 2005, Judge John E. Jones ruled against the Dover Area School Board's policy of requiring biology teachers to read out a statement about ID. Judge Jones stated that ID was religious, not scientific; and that the decision of the Board to adopt this policy, breaching the First Amendment prohibition on state sponsorship of religion, showed 'breathtaking inanity'. Religious leaders have come out against ID too. An open letter affirming the compatibility of Christian faith and the teaching of evolution, first produced in response to controversies in Wisconsin in 2004, has now been signed by over ten thousand clergy from different Christian denominations across America. In 2006, the director of the Vatican Observatory, the Jesuit astronomer George Coyne, condemned ID as a kind of 'crude creationism' which reduced God to a mere engineer.

Given the impressive array of scientific, legal, and theological opinion ranged against it, you might wonder how the ID movement ever became as popular as it undoubtedly has within certain sectors of American society. To answer that question it is necessary to understand the history both of anti-evolution campaigns in the United States since the 1920s and of state and federal courts' use of the First Amendment to keep religion out of public schools from the 1960s onwards. What these histories reveal is that the ID movement is the latest in a series of attempts by a broadly conservative and Christian constituency in the United States to have religiously motivated anti-evolutionary ideas taught in the public schools. The debate about evolution and ID is a conflict not primarily between science and religion but between different views about who should control education.

Opponents of the various forms of scientific creationism and ID have sometimes portrayed them as a 'return to the Middle Ages'. This reveals a common historical misunderstanding. These movements are the products of 20th- and 21st-century America. They simultaneously mimic and reject modern science and have become quite widespread in modern America through the convergent influence of a number of factors, including an advanced state of scientific development, a high level of religious observance, and a strictly enforced separation between church and state.

The Scopes trial

On 21 March 1925, Austin Peay, the Governor of Tennessee, put his signature to an Act making it unlawful for a teacher employed by the State of Tennessee to 'teach any theory that denies the story of the Divine Creation of man as taught in the Bible, and to teach instead that man has descended from a lower order of animals'. Other states, including Mississippi and Arkansas, adopted similar anti-evolution measures in the 1920s, but it was in the small town of Dayton, Tennessee, that the issue came to a head.

The American Civil Liberties Union (ACLU) saw the passing of the Tennessee law as an opportunity to take a stand in defence of intellectual freedom. They placed an advertisement seeking a volunteer to bring a test case. Some of the lawyers and businessmen of Dayton, grasping the opportunity to put their town on the map, persuaded a local science teacher, John Scopes, to put himself forward. What followed generated more publicity than the townsfolk of Dayton can possibly have envisaged. The Dayton 'Monkey Trial' became international news and was the first to be broadcast on national radio. It also attracted two of the most famous lawyers of the age, William Jennings Bryan acting for the prosecution, and Clarence Darrow for the defence. Bryan had stood three times for President, as the candidate of the Democratic Party, and three times had been defeated. Known as 'The Great Commoner' because of his belief in the absolute sovereignty of the people, an opponent of imperialistic foreign policy and supporter of votes for women, in later life Bryan became increasingly taken up with moral and religious crusades, including his support for Prohibition and his biblically based opposition to the teaching of evolution in schools. Darrow was a famous agnostic and a leading member of the ACLU.

The clash between Bryan and Darrow, and the associated carnival of religious and evolutionary activism which descended upon Dayton in July 1925, has been memorably, if not altogether accurately, depicted in the 1960 film *Inherit the Wind*. The story has been brilliantly and more reliably retold by Edward J. Larson in his *Summer for the Gods: The Scopes Trial and America's Continuing Debate over Science and Religion*, which won the Pulitzer Prize for History in 1998. Although the courtroom confrontation between Bryan and Darrow became legendary, as a legal drama it was of limited interest. No-one denied that Scopes had broken the law. Both sides accepted that Scopes had taught evolution, and when the trial came to its conclusion, he was duly convicted and ordered by the judge to pay a fine of 100 dollars. The main purpose of the case, as far as Darrow and the ACLU were concerned, was to obtain a conviction at Dayton which could then be appealed to higher state and federal courts, in order to test the constitutionality of the anti-evolution law. For Bryan, the purpose of convicting Scopes was to strike a political blow for

15. The stall of the Anti-Evolution League in Dayton, Tennessee, during the Scopes trial

honest Christian folk who wanted to shield their children from the anti-religious ideas of an arrogant intellectual elite.

Although some saw the Scopes trial as a simple confrontation between science and religion, the political speeches made by William Jennings Bryan at the time reveal that the more powerful dynamic was a generally conceived conflict between the fundamentals of Christianity and the evils of the modern world. Bryan was a defender of the newly formed movement for Christian 'fundamentalism'. For the fundamentalists, the spread of Darwinism was both a cause and a symptom of the degeneration of human civilization which they witnessed all around them, from the barbaric violence of the First World War in Europe to the sensual decadence of the Jazz Age in America. Christianity and a literal reading of the Bible were bulwarks against these developments. Bryan and others feared that teaching children they were animals would brutalize and degrade them. Bryan noted that in a diagram in Hunter's *Civic Biology*, the textbook from which Scopes had taught evolution, humanity was 'shut up in the little circle entitled "Mammals", with thirty-four hundred and ninety-nine other species':

> Does it not seem a little unfair not to distinguish between man and lower forms of life? What shall we say of the intelligence, not to say religion, of those who are so particular to distinguish between fishes and reptiles and birds, but put a man with an immortal soul in the same circle with the wolf, the hyena and the skunk? What must be the impression made upon children by such a degradation of man?

Bryan and the fundamentalists got what they wanted. In the decades after Scopes was convicted, evolution rarely featured on school science syllabuses, even in states where it was not illegal. On appeal, the Tennessee Supreme Court overturned the conviction not on the constitutional grounds sought by the ACLU but on a technicality. It should have been the jury and not the

16. A fundamentalist cartoon from the 1920s depicting the theory of evolution as the tune played by a new 'Pied Piper' – 'Science falsely so-called' – leading the children of America down the 'path of education' towards the dark cavern of 'disbelief in the God of the Bible'

judge who had set the amount of the fine. It would be another 40 years before an anti-evolution law would finally be challenged in front of the United States Supreme Court.

Varieties of creationism

'Creationism' is a term that can loosely be used to refer to any religious opposition to evolution. Such opposition has taken and continues to take many different forms. What all creationists share is a belief that the universe and life on earth were created immediately and supernaturally by God, and that human beings and all other species were each created separately and in their current form. In other words, creationists deny the common ancestry of all plants and animals. Creationists base their resistance to evolution at least partly on the authority of their sacred text, whether the Hebrew Scriptures, the Christian Bible, or the Quran. The Book of Genesis, for instance, relates that God, over a period of six days, created each kind of living creature separately, made man and woman in his own image, and set them above the rest of creation, before resting on the seventh day. As the King James translation put it:

> And God said, Let us make man in our image, after our likeness: and let them have dominion over the fish of the sea, and over the fowl of the air, and over the cattle, and over all the earth, and over every creeping thing that creepeth upon the earth.

The Quran teaches that Allah is the Creator of everything, bringing the heavens, the earth, and everything in it immediately into existence, and making human beings out of clay and each species separately.

Many creationists have based their stance on a literal interpretation of scripture. Those religious traditions that place a strong emphasis on textual authority, notably some varieties of Protestantism and Islam, are therefore more inclined towards strict creationism. As we have already seen in the case of arguments about Copernican astronomy, however, it is not easy to specify which parts of the scriptures are to be taken absolutely literally. As William Jennings Bryan pointed out during his cross-examination by Clarence Darrow at the Scopes trial, when the Bible said 'Ye are the salt of the earth', the text did not mean that 'man was actually salt or that he had flesh of salt, but it is used in the sense of salt as saving God's people'. That text, Bryan said, was to be 'accepted as it is given', namely 'illustratively' rather than literally. Darrow pressed Bryan further. He wanted to know whether Jonah really had been swallowed by a whale. Bryan corrected him – it was actually a 'big fish'. But, yes, he believed in a God who could make a whale, or a big fish, and a man, and who could 'make both what He pleases'. Darrow moved on to Adam, Eve, and their family. Did Bryan believe that Eve was 'literally made out of Adam's rib'? Bryan said he did. Adam and Eve had two sons, Cain and Abel. But, Darrow wondered, 'Did you ever discover where Cain got his wife?' Bryan was unperturbed: 'No, sir; I leave the agnostics to hunt for her.'

Then Darrow came to questions with obvious scientific relevance. When the Bible said that the sun had been stopped in the sky, did that mean that in those days the sun went round the earth? No, Bryan said, he believed that the earth went round the sun and what the passage meant was that the earth was stopped in its rotation. Then what about the age of the earth? Many bibles had the date 4004 BC printed in the margin to indicate the date of creation, as calculated from the text itself. Did Bryan believe the earth was about six thousand years old? 'Oh, no; I think it is much older than that.' 'How much?' He could not say. What about the six days of creation in Genesis? Were they twenty-four-hour days? Bryan was clear on that one: 'I do not think they were twenty-four-hour days.' Rather, they were 'periods'. God could have taken six days, six years, six million years, or six hundred million years to create the earth. 'I do not think it is important whether we believe one or the other', Bryan said. Soon afterwards, this famous exchange descended into acrimony. Bryan claimed that Darrow was trying to use the courtroom to attack the Bible. Darrow told Bryan he was merely examining 'your fool ideas that no intelligent Christian on earth believes'.

This famous moment during the Scopes trial reveals two important things about creationism generally. First, even among Christian creationists there has been disagreement about how to interpret Genesis. In the early 20th century, many adopted the 'day-age' interpretation favoured by Bryan according to which each biblical 'day' was in fact a geological 'age' during which many different species were created. Others maintained belief in a very ancient earth by inferring a long 'gap' between the first moment of creation and the six-day creation. Within that gap there might have been multiple cataclysms and new creations, responsible for producing the fossil record. 'Young Earth Creationism' or 'Creation Science' is a more extreme version of creationism, according to which the biblical chronology is to be accepted and fossil evidence is to be explained not by successive creations and cataclysms but entirely as the result of Noah's flood, approximately five thousand years ago. The Creation Science movement's key texts, second only to the Bible in importance, were works by the Seventh-Day Adventist geologist George McCready Price. His *Illogical Geology: The Weakest Point in the Evolution Theory* (1906) and *New Geology* (1923) both explained geological evidence by a recent universal deluge.

Price's books were the inspiration for the Creation Science revival of the 1960s and 1970s, led by a Texan Baptist teacher of civil engineering, Henry M. Morris. The Creation Research Society was founded by Morris in 1963, and the Institute for Creation Research in 1970. Both were designed to promote a more extreme and allegedly more scientific form of fundamentalist creationism than had ever existed before. As with Bryan's anti-evolution campaign, the core motivation for the Creation Science movement was a desire to protect Christian communities from the corrosive and degenerate influences of the modern world. The range of evils thought to grow out of a belief in evolution in the 1970s were graphically illustrated in R. G. Elmendorf's 'Evolution Tree', which bore fruit ranging widely from secularism, socialism, and relativism to alcohol, 'dirty books', 'homosex', and even terrorism. This brand of anti-evolutionary thought has spread from America around the world. In recent years an Islamic author from Turkey writing under the pen-name of Harun Yayha has produced many widely read books denouncing Darwinism as a 'deceit' and a

THE EVOLUTION TREE

Evolution is not just a "harmless biological theory" - it produces evil fruit. Evolution is the supposedly "scientific" rationale for all kinds of unbiblical ideas which permeate society today and concern many people. Evolution "holds up" these ideas, and if evolution is destroyed, these ideas will fall.

The "kingdom" of evolution starts with a small no-god biological idea sown in the fertile ground of unbelief. Nourished by sin, it grows up into a "tree", sending out "great branches" into education, government, medicine, religion and so forth, and eventually covering the "whole world". Then all sorts of evil ideas come and "lodge in the branches thereof" (Matthew 13/31-32, Mark 4/31-32):

PHILOSOPHICAL

HUMANISM
ABORTION
ALCOHOL
Medicine
CULTS
HOMOSEX
Law
COMMUNISM
SEX EDUCATION
Business
Science
SUICIDE
GENETIC ENG'G
Economics
DRUGG
RELATIVISM
Music
RACISM
WOM/CHILD LIB
DIRTY BOOKS
Politics
Literature
MORAL EDUCATION
INFLATION
HARD ROCK
SOCIALISM
Education
Religion
TERRORISM
SECULARISM
CRIME
Government
Art
Military

EVOLUTION

GENERAL PUBLIC

MANY CHRISTIANS

"A good tree cannot bring forth evil fruit; neither can a corrupt tree bring forth good fruit" Matthew 7/18

BIOLOGICAL EVOLUTION

"Science falsely so-called" (I Tim 6/20)

SCIENTIFIC CREATIONISM

SIN

NO GOD

SIN

SIN

SIN

SIN

SIN

UNBELIEF

What is the best way to counteract the evil fruit of evolution? Opposing these things one-by-one is good, but it does not deal with the underlying cause. The tree will produce fruit faster than it can be spotted and removed. A more effective approach is to chop the tree off at its base by scientifically discrediting evolution. When the tree falls, the fruit will go down with it, and unbelieving man will be left "without excuse" (Romans 1/21). That is the real reason why scientific creationism represents such a serious threat to the evolutionary establishment!

Pittsburgh Creation Society
Bairdford Pa 15006
R G Elmendorf

17. A creationist image of the 1970s: the 'Evolution Tree' is nourished by sin and unbelief, and its fruits include a range of secular ideologies, immoral activities, and economic and social evils.

'lie' and drawing on the techniques and arguments of American proponents of Creation Science.

The second general feature of creationism illustrated by Bryan's testimony is its ambivalent relationship with science. The reason Bryan accepted that the earth orbited the sun and that it was much more than six thousand years old was because of the scientific evidence to that effect. Why, then, was he committed to the belief that Eve had literally been made from Adam's rib, and that the Genesis account of creation was to be preferred to evolutionary science? At what point does the creationist stop believing the scientific evidence and start taking the Bible literally? And why? The answer in practice is, as we have already seen, that it has been the question of human evolution that has caused greatest unease, and it is at the suggestion of animal ancestry for humans that most creationists have felt they must draw the line.

Creationist ambivalence towards science is evident in other ways too. Many creationists, while resisting certain scientific results, specifically relating to evolution, still admire the success of science and seek to emulate or even appropriate that success. The recasting of fundamentalist anti-evolution as an alternative kind of science by Morris and the Creation Scientists was partly motivated by the desire to have creationism taught in the public schools as an alternative to evolutionary science. However, Price, whose geological works provided the scientific basis of their movement, wrote at a time before that had become the real issue. He genuinely wished to produce an understanding of nature that was both biblical and scientific.

One of the most popular books about Islam and science in the 20th century was *The Bible, The Quran and Science* by the Muslim physician Maurice Bucaille. Published in 1976, the book claimed that the word of God as revealed in the Quran (but not the Bible) contained many statements that could only be understood in the light of modern science. Bucaille started a craze among Islamic commentators for finding verses in the Quran that seemed to foreshadow scientific discoveries as diverse as the expansion of the universe and the mechanisms of sexual reproduction. Other Islamic scholars, while rejecting both Bucaille's anachronistic hunt for modern science in the Quran and also Yayha's second-hand creationism, still seek a way to produce an 'Islamic science' which is truly scientific and yet which is divorced from purely materialistic interpretations incompatible with the Quran.

The First Amendment

Intelligent Design is not strictly speaking a form of creationism. Proponents of ID do not mention the Bible, let alone try to interpret it literally, and do not explain geological and fossil evidence in terms of a biblical flood. They accept the antiquity of the earth and of humanity, and in the case of some really liberal ID theorists, such as Michael Behe, do not even deny the common ancestry of humans and all other forms of life. Behe accepts more or less all of the standard evolutionary picture but identifies certain key phenomena, such as the biochemistry of the first cells, which he insists cannot be explained without the intervention of an intelligent designer. Other proponents of ID claim that the 'Cambrian explosion' of new complex forms of life about five hundred and thirty million years ago is inexplicable without intelligent intervention. The defenders of ID, to an even greater extent than the 'Creation Scientists' of previous decades, try to stay scrupulously within the bounds of scientific discourse and mention a 'designer' and 'intelligence', but never God, and certainly not the Bible. Some suspect that this reflects not the scientific nature of their enterprise but simply a canny awareness of the fact that they will need to look and sound as much like scientists as possible if their views are ever going to make it into the classrooms of America's public schools.

The Establishment Clause of the First Amendment to the US Constitution forbids the government from passing any law 'respecting an establishment of religion'. The original intention was not to exclude religion from public life altogether but to ensure that no particular form of Christianity become an established religion akin to the Church of England. There was also from the outset a broader hope that this Amendment would help to build, in the words of Thomas Jefferson, 'a wall of separation between Church and state'. The enactment of statutes forbidding state employees from contradicting the 'story of the Divine Creation of man as taught in the Bible' would seem on the face of it to put something of a hole in that wall.

From the middle of the 20th century onwards, the US Supreme Court became increasingly active in policing the observation of the Establishment Clause in publicly funded schools. State laws allowing time for silent prayer in schools, or for the reading of denominationally neutral prayers, or requiring the Ten Commandments to be posted on classroom walls were all declared unconstitutional. In the 1960s, an anti-evolution law from the Scopes era was finally challenged on similar constitutional grounds. A young biology teacher from Arkansas, Susan Epperson, supported by the ACLU, challenged a 1928 state law making it unlawful to teach 'the theory or doctrine that mankind ascended or descended from a lower order of animals'. The case went all the way to the US Supreme Court, which ruled that the law was in violation of the First Amendment. The Court declared, in November 1968, that 'fundamentalist sectarian conviction was and is the law's reason for existence'. The Epperson case marked the beginning of the legal process which would give rise to the Intelligent Design movement about 20 years later.

In the 1970s, the creationist camp adopted a new strategy, campaigning for legislation mandating 'balanced treatment' or 'equal time' in the classroom for two alternative scientific theories – 'evolution science' and versions of Morris's 'Creation Science', which did not mention the Bible but asserted a separate ancestry for man and apes, a 'relatively recent inception of the earth and living kinds', and an explanation of geology by 'catastrophism, including a worldwide flood'. These measures did not stay long on the statute books. The Arkansas balanced treatment law was struck down at state level in 1982, on First Amendment grounds. In 1987, a similar law passed by the State of Louisiana came before the US Supreme Court. The Court ruled that the statute's purported secular aim of promoting academic freedom was a sham and that its real purpose was to 'advance the religious viewpoint that a supernatural being created humankind'. Because the primary aim of the Louisiana Act was to 'endorse a particular religious doctrine', it was in violation of the Establishment Clause of the First Amendment.

So, at the beginning of the 1990s, biblical anti-evolution laws had been declared unconstitutional; laws requiring 'balanced treatment' for evolution and 'Creation Science' had gone the same way; but opinion polls continued to find that between 45 and 50% of the population of the USA believed that human beings were created by God in their present form at some time in the last ten thousand years. (This figure remains the same today, with most of the rest of the population believing that humanity evolved through an evolutionary process somehow guided by God.) Legislators and members of school boards seeking to tap into the support of these voters now needed to develop a new strategy for getting God back into the classroom in scientific clothing. And that explains the birth of the 'Intelligent Design' movement. School boards and state legislatures across the US have considered measures introducing ID into science education. Judge Jones's ruling in 2005, which struck down the Dover School Board's policy on First Amendment grounds, because of the clear religious intention behind it, strongly suggests that ID will have no more legal success than previous kinds of religiously motivated anti-Darwinism. The First Amendment will continue to do its job.

In 1925, William Jennings Bryan saw that the central political question to be decided was 'Who shall control our public schools?' Debates about ID continue to bring out the social conflicts that arise in trying to answer that question. Bryan said that an evolutionist school teacher should not be allowed 'to accept employment in a Christian community and teach that the Bible is untrue' and to 'force his opinion upon students against the wishes of the taxpayers and the parents'. Bryan predicted that 'school board elections may become the most important elections held, for parents are much more interested in their children and in their children's religion than they are in any political policies'. In many parts of the USA Bryan's prediction came true. In some cases, the decisions of the courts to strike down creationist laws did indeed go against the wishes of parents and taxpayers. But, as Judge William Overton stated in ruling against the Arkansas 'balanced treatment' Act in 1982, 'The application and content of First Amendment principles are not determined by public opinion polls or by a majority vote.' No group, no matter how large or small, was allowed to 'use the organs of government, of which the public schools are the most conspicuous and influential, to foist its religious beliefs on others'.

Things have changed since Bryan's day, however. In recent years, it has been the democratic process itself rather than the courts which has done most to keep ID off science syllabuses. In Dover and elsewhere, members of school boards who have changed science standards to de-emphasize evolution or to include references to ID have generally been voted out at the next election. Was Bryan right after all, that it is best to let parents and taxpayers have the final say through the ballot box?

Explaining complexity

But suppose that the courts and the people were not opposed to the teaching of ID, or that the question of whether ID might be taught in science classes were to arise in a country lacking the strict separation between state and religion enforced in the United States. What then? It would still be very unlikely that many people would consider ID a sensible subject for a science lesson. Good scientific, theological, and educational objections to such a proposal would be plentiful.

Starting with the scientific case against ID, there are two related points to make. First, evolutionary theory can in fact explain the biological complexity which ID claims defeats it; second, ID is excessively negative, looking for gaps in evolutionary science but without providing a coherent alternative theory in its place.

Arguments about 'irreducible complexity' are a new form of a very old anti-Darwinian argument, namely that complex structures could not have evolved by natural selection because the intermediate forms containing only some of the parts would not have been adaptive. What use is a part of an eye, half a wing, or three-quarters of a flagellum? In general terms, evolutionists have been able to answer this objection by finding, either in fossils or in living species, evidence of intermediate structures that did exist and were in fact adaptive. In the case of the eye, Darwin himself listed various forms of eyes, from a small patch of light-sensitive cells to the complex 'camera' eyes of humans and other animals, showing how each was adaptive and could have evolved into the next in the series. Scientists now estimate that this entire evolutionary process could even have been achieved within a mere half a million years. Advantages were also conferred by the precursors to fully fledged wings. Feathers, for instance, seem first to have evolved as a form of insulation before being co-opted by natural selection to aid a quite different function – flight. It is harder to produce these scenarios in the case of biochemistry because, obviously, chemical reactions, unlike feathers, do not fossilize. However, using evidence from currently living species it is possible to reconstruct evolutionary scenarios. This has been done, for instance, in the case of the famous bacterial flagellum, which, it has been suggested, evolved through the co-option of a very similar existing structure (known as the type three secretory system) used by bacteria for injecting toxic proteins into the cells of their hosts. So the answer to the question 'What use is a part of an eye, half a wing, or three-quarters of a flagellum?', is 'Light-detection, warmth, and toxin-injection, respectively'.

A second objection to ID concerns its negative character. This is another respect in which ID differs from Scientific Creationism. Creationists of earlier decades proposed an alternative theory which boldly, biblically, and patently wrongly asserted that the earth was only a few thousand years old, that geology could be explained by a recent worldwide flood, and that humans did not share ancestors with other animals. The defenders of ID, on the other hand, simply draw attention to what they claim are phenomena (such as the Cambrian explosion or the blood clotting cascade) that display too much 'specified complexity' to have evolved by mutation and natural selection, and at that point invoke their unelaborated concept of an intelligent designer, barring the way to further investigation. The ID theory makes no novel predictions beyond the failure of evolutionary science to explain these phenomena. It is not clear where ID theorists would draw the line between that which can be explained by evolution and that which needs an intelligent designer. And it seems likely that, in future, as good evolutionary explanations are suggested for their favoured examples, as has already happened in the case of the flagellum, the number of cases for which 'design' can be claimed will slowly but surely dwindle.

One of the main theological objections to ID follows directly from this last point. In claiming that supernatural intervention is required to explain a certain subset of natural phenomena for which a full evolutionary explanation may currently be lacking, ID theorists seem to be positing a 'God of the gaps' of the kind discussed in Chapter 3. As gaps in evolutionary science are filled with naturalistic explanations, God will gradually be edged further out. This tinkering God of ID, this God who seems to be an occasionally observable object in the natural world, found in our current ignorance rather than in our understanding, is no more attractive to theologians than to scientists – hence the thousands of clergy who have been moved to sign the open letter against ID mentioned above.

But is it science?

Judge Overton in the 1982 Arkansas case and Judge Jones in the 2005 case in Pennsylvania both declared that Creation Science and ID, respectively, not only contravened the First Amendment but were, in any case, not proper science. This is a common claim – that creationism and ID are not scientific because they fail to fulfil one or more criteria which characterize all genuine science. There are various candidates for such 'demarcation criteria'. Some say that true science must be empirically testable, others that it must make 'falsifiable' claims, others that it must offer explanations only in terms of natural laws and natural processes.

Philosophers of science are much less optimistic than they were a few decades ago about the possibility of finding any really coherent demarcation criteria. It is accepted that many scientific claims – including many of the most interesting ones – are not directly empirically testable but only become so as part of a complex network of auxiliary theoretical assumptions and scientific instruments. For instance, a mathematical model of the Big Bang cannot be tested by direct observation, but only indirectly through predictions about the behaviour of measuring apparatus when a particular reaction is set off in a massive particle accelerator. Creation Scientists made very clearly testable claims about the age of the earth and the separate ancestry of all species. Although it is an unusually minimal and largely negative kind of theory, ID certainly can generate empirically testable claims too, such as the assertion that adaptive precursors will never be found for various specified processes and structures such as the blood clotting cascade or the bacterial flagellum. Creationists and ID proponents have regularly made testable claims. These claims have been tested and repeatedly found wanting.

It is also accepted that good scientists will often hold on to their theories in the face of inconsistent empirical evidence and seek to reinterpret that evidence rather than declare their theory 'falsified'. There is not yet an evolutionary account which successfully identifies every single stage in the evolution of the flagellum (or in the evolutionary history of many other organs or biochemical processes), but that does not mean that scientists should declare neo-Darwinism to have been 'falsified'. The modern framework of evolutionary theory successfully explains and unifies a huge body of evidence accumulated and interpreted over many generations. It makes sense of the fossil record, the geographical distribution of species, the physical similarities between related plants and animals, and the vestigial organs that testify to earlier evolutionary forms. Recent advances in genetic sequencing have provided a huge new mass of evidence which confirms evolutionary theory while identifying a whole new range of puzzles and anomalies. In the face of puzzles and anomalies a good scientist, especially when working with such a well-confirmed theory, does not declare their theory falsified, but designs new experiments and develops new theoretical models to solve those puzzles and resolve those anomalies. The central claims of ID theorists all seem to have been falsified. But in holding on to their theories and trying to provide an alternative interpretation of the evidence, they are only doing what all good scientists would do. A very significant difference, however, is that ID supporters lack any good reason for confidence in their original theory.

Testability and falsifiability are not satisfactory demarcation criteria. What about the insistence that proper scientific theories should be entirely naturalistic? This is a relatively new doctrine.

Neither Isaac Newton nor Charles Darwin, to take just two examples, felt that God had to be excluded entirely from their scientific accounts of the natural world. In scientific theories between the 17th and 19th centuries, God featured generally as a lawgiver rather than as a tinkerer, but God was not absolutely barred from professional scientific discourse until the later 19th century. In appealing to a supernatural cause as part of their science in the 21st century, ID theorists are certainly unconventional, eccentric, and out of step with recent practice, but that need not mean they are to be excluded from the realm of science altogether. There is no need for defenders of mainstream science to risk seeming ideological and doctrinaire by prejudging the kinds of entities that will feature in successful scientific theories in the future.

In short, opponents of ID who use the weapon of philosophical demarcation may be shooting themselves quite unnecessarily in the foot. In the United States, the pro-religious intent and effect of any policy mandating the teaching of creationism or ID will be enough to keep it off the statute book. There and elsewhere, scientists and theologians, as well as voters and judges, also have many good reasons to resist ID without straying into the fraught philosophical realm of demarcation.

Back to the classroom

The most recent slogan of the ID movement, echoing the calls for 'balanced treatment' of earlier decades, is 'Teach the Controversy'. The publisher's description of the ID textbook *Of Pandas and People* states that it 'promotes a widely recognized goal of science education by fostering a questioning, skeptical and scrutinizing mindset'. Other ID proponents claim they are seeking to improve public discussions of science and promote a more inclusive and 'controversy-based biology curriculum'. This is disingenuous. Of course science thrives on constant criticism, questioning, and controversy. Such controversies can be a very useful way to teach science. To the extent that ID theorists have served as gadflies or catalysts to evolutionary science, they have performed a valuable scientific function. However, ID is not really a movement for educational reform. The 'controversy' in question has not arisen from any substantial scientific disagreement but is the product of a concerted public relations exercise aimed at the Christian parents of America.

Even if we are charitable and allow that ID might be a kind of science, it is a dreadfully obscure and unsuccessful kind of science. If, in the future, ID became the basis of a serious and fruitful scientific research programme and thus converted a substantial proportion of the scientific community to its views, then it might be reasonable to discuss the inclusion of ID on a science curriculum (if First Amendment objections could somehow be overcome). At the moment, ID is supported by a tiny handful of very marginal scientific figures, is rejected by the rest of the scientific world, and appeals to a wider public for patently religious reasons. There is an almost endless list of interesting scientific and philosophical controversies that would be candidates for inclusion on a 'controversy-based biology curriculum'. But many would be excluded because they were too technically demanding, too far removed from mainstream science, or too clearly manufactured by a special-interest group for political and ideological reasons. The debate about ID would fail on all three counts. In addition to the political, legal, scientific, and theological reasons for excluding ID from science classes, then, there are perfectly good educational ones too.

There is no genuine scientific controversy about the relative merits of evolution and ID. But creationism and ID do draw attention to genuinely controversial questions about the nature of science and its place in society: Should voters, elected politicians, judges, or scientific experts have the final say about what is taught in the science classes of publicly funded schools? Why has modern America proved such fertile ground for the growth of anti-evolutionary movements? Can God ever be discovered through scientific methods? Can testability, falsifiability, naturalism, or any combination of these, be invoked as viable demarcation criteria? Wherever comparative religion and the history and philosophy of science are taught, creationism and ID can profitably be studied. Indeed, if the effect of the continued exclusion of ID from the science syllabus is that its advocates start a campaign for the inclusion of these other subjects on the curricula of publicly funded schools, then some educational good may still come out of this peculiarly American controversy.

Chapter 6
Mind and morality

We have seen that religious responses to evolution in all traditions continue to centre on questions about human nature. How can human beings be created in God's image, believers ask, but also be nothing more than improved apes with mushrooms for cousins? If human beings have physically evolved from lower forms of life, then at what point, if any, did the rational soul develop? Since the 19th century, scientific studies of the brain and mind have been providing further challenges to religious beliefs. If the soul is nothing but a product of brain activity, as science seems to suggest, does that not imply materialism, determinism, blank atheism? What place does such a view leave for belief in moral responsibility in this life or the prospect of rewards or punishments in the next?

For many people, it is these questions about mind and morality that drive the whole debate about science and religion. Believers resist the idea that human consciousness, morality, and even religion itself can be explained scientifically. If religious experience and human morality can be explained as natural phenomena, there seems to be no further need for supernatural accounts of such things. And those who promote such explanations often do so as part of an explicit campaign to show both that religious beliefs are mistaken and that science can explain their real origins.

This chapter asks what the implications really are of the scientific study of mind and morality. It also asks what ethical significance, if any, can be attached to scientific claims that human behaviours including altruism and homosexuality are natural. It ends by suggesting that science and medicine seem to have stepped into roles that were previously the preserve of religion, by defining and enforcing divisions between the normal and the deviant, and by using visions of the future to alter our behaviour in the present.

The soul and immortality

When scientists started to turn their attention to the human mind they were approaching a domain that had for many centuries been at the centre of religious life and thought. Not all religions include reverence for sacred scriptures, nor even belief in a creator God, but all religious traditions, East and West, teach that wisdom and salvation are to be found in the life of the mind.

Different words are used to refer to those sensations, thoughts, and emotions that are so central to the religious life. Historically the terms 'mind' and 'soul' have been the most generally adopted, sometimes used synonymously and sometimes with one being a subset of the other. 'Self', 'spirit', and 'consciousness' can similarly denote either a general or a more specific aspect of mental life. In the specialist literature there is little consensus about the exact meaning of these terms. However, it is certainly the case that the realities to which they refer are of particular religious concern. Religions teach individuals how to use spiritual exercises such as meditation and prayer, as well as ritual and liturgy, to achieve a state of greater enlightenment, spiritual awareness, and moral and religious strength. They also teach that each individual has a soul, the state and eternal destiny of which will be determined by their actions in this life.

There is a great variety of teachings about immortality, resurrection, rebirth, transmigration, or reincarnation that feature in various traditions. There are many disagreements and differences of emphasis even within and between the three monotheistic traditions, but there are some common elements that we can pick out. Judaism, Christianity, and Islam all teach that there will be some kind of life after death, and that it will take the form of either a bodily resurrection, the survival of a disembodied soul, or both. They also all teach that the nature of the afterlife will depend on one's spiritual state. There will be a moment of judgement in which God will divide humanity into two categories, which are variously conceived of as the elect and the damned, the faithful and the faithless, or the righteous and the wicked. The chosen ones will spend an eternity of peace and joy with God, the unfortunate remainder will be punished. According to traditional interpretations of Christian and Muslim teachings, those who are not among God's chosen will be consigned eternally to a hellish fiery pit. Ideas about hell have been less prominent in Judaism. According to some Jewish teachers, punishments in hell are only a temporary prelude to eternal bliss. In those traditions in which God does make a final and irreversible judgement between the elect and the damned, the exact basis of the division depends on whether it is God's will, religious faith, or good works that is supposed to be the decisive criterion. Even those who emphasize the inscrutability of the divine will for each soul, or the importance of faith over works, would generally hold that God's chosen ones will be righteous in this life, even if that righteousness is not itself the reason for their salvation. The important point is that religious belief in a future life has always been intimately connected with the ethical and social question of how to live in this one.

Brain and mind

That the brain is the organ of the mind has become increasingly apparent through modern scientific research. This discovery has led some to question traditional beliefs about the existence of an immortal soul and the possibility of an afterlife.

Nineteenth-century attempts to specify the exact nature of the connection between brain and mind included the science of 'craniology' or 'phrenology', according to which the extent of the development of different sections of the brain could be discerned from the shape of someone's skull. The different parts of the brain under the 'bumps' on the skull were correlated with different mental traits, such as love of children, secretiveness, self-esteem, and so on. Phrenologists could thus tell people what the shape of their head revealed about their mental capacities. It became a popular craze for a while in Victorian Britain and functioned as a sort of neurological version of reading one's horoscope. People were fascinated to be told about what their bumps revealed about their character traits and their future destinies, by those with a special understanding of the secret workings of nature. Queen Victoria even arranged for her children to be given phrenological readings.

Although the details of phrenology were all wrong, the basic idea that different mental functions were correlated with particular parts of the brain turned out to be a scientifically fruitful one. Studying patients who had suffered brain damage, through disease or injury, allowed scientists to start to make more accurate statements about localization. In the 1860s, the French physician Paul Broca discovered the area – still known as 'Broca's area' – in the frontal lobes of the brain that was responsible for speech production. The extraordinary case of Phineas Gage provided further insights. Gage was a railroad construction worker in the state of Vermont in the USA. In an accident in September 1848, Gage was injured by a metre-long iron tamping rod, which was driven by a dynamite blast through his cheek and out of the top of his head. Astonishingly, Gage survived with his faculties apparently intact. But it soon became clear that the damage to his frontal lobes had produced a powerful change in his personality. He had lost the ability to empathize with others, and his social behaviour became unpredictable and erratic. Gage's story is just one very memorable example among the thousands of cases

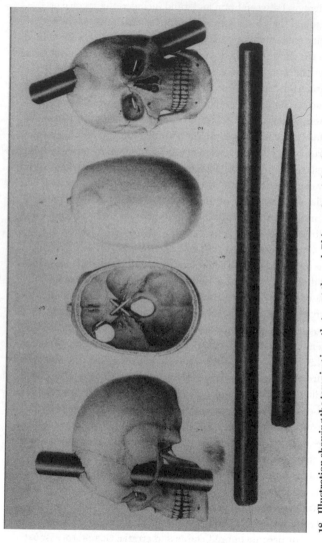

18. Illustration showing the tamping iron that went through Phineas Gage's head in 1848, and the route that it took through his skull

through which an ever more detailed understanding of the functions of different brain areas has emerged.

The invention in more recent times of brain scanning technologies has allowed this project to be pursued with greater precision, revealing the dynamic interactions of different parts of the brain, and offering insights into the working of intact brains as well as damaged ones. Neuroscientists can even use magnetic fields to stimulate parts of the brain experimentally and study the mental effects on their intrepid subjects. These techniques have all been applied specifically to religious experiences as well as to many other mental capacities. Buddhist monks and Roman Catholic nuns these days seem to be in constant danger of being asked by neuroscientists to insert themselves into an fMRI (functional Magnetic Resonance Imaging) scanner or to don a special rubber cap wired up with electrodes, all in the service of the neuroscientific study of spiritual experiences.

Some of these studies have suggested that there are particular parts of the brain that are especially involved in religious experiences. One candidate has been the temporal lobes, partly on the basis of the apparent susceptibility to religious experiences of sufferers of temporal lobe epilepsy. The American neuroscientist Michael Persinger has taken this idea a step further by creating a device to stimulate that part of the brain in an attempt to induce religious experiences in experimental subjects. His 'Transcranial Magnetic Stimulator', or 'God helmet' as others have called it, was applied with disputed results. But many who participated in the experiment reported feelings of a numinous presence or transcendent oneness. Other studies have identified different brain areas as being especially involved in meditative states. And some recent work suggests there is no single 'God spot'. A study of Carmelite nuns carried out in 2006 by Mario Beauregard and Vincent Paquette, for example, found that several different brain areas were simultaneously involved in their spiritual experiences.

Dualism and physicalism

What are the implications of this scientific research for religion? One newspaper report of Beauregard and Paquette's study ran under the headline: 'Nuns Prove God Is Not Figment of the Mind'. The somewhat tortuous idea behind the headline seemed to be that if the whole brain is involved in religious experiences then that contradicts the theory that there is one special 'God spot', perhaps in the temporal lobes, and with it the associated belief that religious experiences are 'nothing but' the activation of that one brain area. Why it would be any less religiously or theologically troubling to find that spiritual feelings were produced by the activation of many parts of the brain, rather than just one, is not clear. This is a good example of the theological and philosophical ambiguity of empirical neuroscientific studies.

The success of neuroscience in showing that there are correlations between certain states of the brain and certain associated mental experiences, including religious ones, has been interpreted by some as a direct refutation of traditional beliefs about mystical experiences and the immortality of the soul. According to this sceptical stance, an experience can be caused by the brain or by an immaterial being (God or the soul) but not both: a neurological explanation of an experience rules out a supernatural or religious one. Science has explained away the supernatural.

That might seem a reasonable and simple enough assumption. However, there are plenty of philosophers, scientists, and theologians who would deny it. To offer neurological or, for that matter, evolutionary explanations of where our religious and moral beliefs come from is an interesting scientific enterprise. It flourishes today as one part of the ambitious programme of research known as 'Cognitive Science'. But since absolutely all our beliefs – religious, scientific, or otherwise – are, on this hypothesis, the products of the same evolved neurological apparatus, drawing attention to that fact does not get us any further forward in the philosophical endeavour of distinguishing between the true ones and the false ones.

Another response to the perceived challenge of neuroscience to religious belief has been to adopt a form of 'dualism' – in other words, to assert that there exist two distinct kinds of substance, or properties, the mental and the physical, which interact with each other, especially in human beings. The dualist would interpret the close correlations discovered by neuroscientists as evidence not that the mind is nothing but brain activity, but rather that the mind interacts with the brain, or uses the brain as its instrument. René Descartes's 17th-century version of this philosophy is the one that has received most scholarly attention, but there are plenty of modern successors to his view, both among philosophers and more widely. Key problems in making sense of dualism include the question of how the physical and the non-physical can causally interact with each other, and explaining why dualism is to be preferred to the apparently simpler alternative of physicalism, according to which mental properties are properties of the brain.

Even if all mental experience is, in some sense, physical, it is still not straightforward to articulate what that sense is. Why is it that particular bits of matter (exclusively, as far as we know, complex networks of nerve cells within the brains of living animals) exhibit the properties of consciousness and others (such as rocks, vegetables, or even computers) do not? Philosophers and theologians interested in this question have, in recent years, discussed concepts such as 'emergence', 'supervenience', and 'non-reductive physicalism', all of which try to articulate how mental realities can be both dependent on and yet autonomous from the physical. To say that the mind is 'emergent' or 'supervenient' is to suggest it is autonomous, not in the sense of being able to exist independently of the brain, but in the sense that it exhibits properties and regularities that are not susceptible to systematic reduction to the neurological level.

Bodily resurrection and subjective immortality

For most believers, I imagine, it would be a step too far beyond the teachings of their tradition to accept an entirely physicalist reinterpretation of 'mind' and 'soul'. There are, however, resources in those traditions that might support such an approach. The Hebrew Bible offers a much more embodied idea of human personhood than that developed later under the influence of Greek philosophies, which tended to emphasize the duality of body and mind. In the Book of Genesis, in punishing Adam and Eve for their disobedience in the Garden of Eden, God says to Adam, 'By the sweat of your brow you will eat your food until you return to the ground, since from it you were taken; for dust you are and to dust you will return.' This same language is echoed by the preacher in the Book of Ecclesiastes: 'For the fate of the sons of men and the fate of the beasts is the same; as one dies, so dies the other. They all have the same breath, and man has no advantage over the beasts; for all is vanity. All go to one place; all are from the dust, and all turn to dust again.' St Paul's writings in the New Testament also emphasize bodily resurrection more than the immortality of the soul, and the Apostles', Nicene, and Athanasian Creeds affirm belief, respectively, in 'the resurrection of the body and the life everlasting', 'the resurrection of the dead and the life everlasting', and the view that at Christ's second coming 'all men shall rise again with their bodies and shall give account of their own works'.

To return to a more traditional belief in bodily resurrection rather than spiritual immortality is, in one way, an elegant religious solution to the problem of how to respond to advances in neuroscience. However, the effect really is to go from a dualistic frying pan into an apocalyptic fire. If modern science suggests that belief in an immortal soul is problematic, it might equally, to say the least, question the evidential basis for the notion that at some point in the future God will bring history to an end in a final eschatological act in which the universe will be destroyed and recreated and the dead will be brought back in bodily form to be judged by their maker. For those who prefer this one huge miracle to the problems raised by trying to find a place for an immaterial soul in the history of human evolution and in the activities of the brain, belief in physicalism and a bodily resurrection might continue to seem the most acceptable option nonetheless.

And for those who cannot believe in either a spiritual rebirth or a physical resurrection, there is perhaps some comfort in the idea of subjective immortality – the humanist notion that the selfish desire for heavenly rewards in a future life should be replaced by a more humble hope that one might live on after death through one's friends, one's children, or one's work. This ancient idea was popular among secularists in the 19th century, and was expressed in the closing lines of George Eliot's novel *Middlemarch* (1871–2). The narrator, speaking of the book's heroine Dorothea, says:

> the effect of her being on those around her was incalculably diffusive: for the growing good of the world is partly dependent on unhistoric acts; and that things are not so ill with you and me as they might have been, is half owing to the number who lived faithfully a hidden life, and rest in unvisited tombs.

But not everyone likes the idea. When asked if he hoped to achieve immortality through the impact of his films, Woody Allen replied: 'I don't want to achieve immortality through my work. I want to achieve it through not dying.'

Selfishness and altruism

As we have already seen, beliefs about the soul and the afterlife have always been closely connected with concerns about morality and social life in the here and now. That connection has sometimes been made very crudely and explicitly. A popular book of *Divine and Moral Songs for Children* composed in the 18th century by the Congregationalist clergyman Isaac Watts contained the following poem about the link between holy living and heavenly rewards, which would have been recited by many generations of British children:

There is beyond the sky
   A heaven of joy and love;
And holy children, when they die,
   Go to that world above.

There is a dreadful hell,
   And everlasting pains:
There sinners must with devils dwell
   In darkness, fire, and chains.

Can such a wretch as I
   Escape this cursed end?
And may I hope, whene'er I die,
   I shall to heaven ascend?

Then will I read and pray,
   While I have life and breath,
Lest I should be cut off today,
   And sent t' eternal death.

When freethinking and anti-Christian works such as Thomas Paine's *Age of Reason* (1794) started to become more widely available, one of the leading concerns of the faithful was that if people ceased to believe in heaven and hell, then they would feel free to indulge their most sensual passions and selfish appetites. Without religion, it was feared, human society would descend into animalistic anarchy. As one judge said when sentencing a London bookseller to imprisonment for selling Paine's works, if these books were widely read and believed then the law would be deprived of 'one of its principal sanctions – the dread of future punishments'.

Many today still echo the sentiments of this 18th-century judge and argue that religious beliefs are necessary to provide moral guidance and standards of virtuous conduct in an otherwise corrupt, materialistic, and degenerate world. Religions certainly do provide a framework within which people can learn the difference between right and wrong. An individual might consult the scriptures to discover that God has told his people to be truthful, faithful, and respectful towards their parents; and not to steal, nor commit adultery, nor worship false gods. Believers can also hope to receive moral guidance from the voice of God within, in the form of their conscience. If they follow the divine path faithfully, they will be deemed to be among the righteous rather than the wicked at the day of judgement. The unbeliever, in contrast, is supposed to be a sensuous, self-indulgent, selfish creature whose motto is 'Let us eat and drink; for tomorrow we die.'

The alleged connection between unbelief and selfishness has been strengthened by a particular interpretation of evolution as a process driven by self-assertion and competition. Standard modern explanations of evolution have emphasized the fact that a trait or behaviour cannot evolve unless it is for the good of the individual organism. This would seem to rule out the possibility of altruism (except as a sort of enlightened self-interest). If evolution cannot produce genuine altruism, then perhaps the only explanation for the self-sacrifice displayed by saintly individuals is that they are inspired or empowered by God. Even the former director of the Human Genome Project, Francis Collins, in his book *The Language of God* (2006), suggests that the existence of the 'moral law' of love and altruism within every human heart cannot be explained by science alone.

This might be another occasion, however, where it would be wise for religious apologists to heed Henry Drummond's warning about not placing God in supposed gaps in existing knowledge. For many, this particular alleged gap was filled some time ago. Darwin himself suggested that cooperative behaviour could arise through natural selection operating at the level of tribes or groups. A community made up of cooperative and self-sacrificing individuals would be expected to flourish at the expense of one made up of uncooperative and selfish ones. In his 1976 book *The Selfish Gene*, Richard Dawkins popularized an alternative evolutionary explanation of altruism – the theory of 'kin selection', which asserts that altruism could arise only when individuals were acting in the interests of family members. Since, according to this version of neo-Darwinism, natural selection operates at the level of the gene, we could only come to behave in an altruistic way when it was in the interest of our 'selfish genes'. And that was only the case when we were helping to spread more copies of those genes by aiding close relatives (who share many of the same genes). A gene that inclined us to help non-relatives, on the other hand, would have no such evolutionary advantage since it would succeed only in spreading copies of unrelated, competing genes.

Of course, Dawkins did not intend to attribute any kind of actual intention – selfish or otherwise – to the genes themselves. His imaginative and metaphorical application of the term 'selfish' to strings of DNA molecules was, rather, designed to communicate a complex scientific theory to a wide readership. In that aim, Dawkins succeeded brilliantly. One unfortunate side-effect was the degree of confusion he thus introduced into debates about altruism. In a rhetorical flourish in *The Selfish Gene*, Dawkins wrote, 'Let us try to *teach* generosity and altruism, because we are born selfish.' However, the whole point of the theory of kin selection is that individuals can behave entirely altruistically (in the normal non-molecular sense of the word), but the reason they do so is because it helps to spread their genes. The real point of the book is that 'selfish' genes can make altruistic people. But Dawkins's reference to the need for us to 'rebel against the tyranny of the selfish replicators' and to teach our children altruism rather obscured this point. In his recent book, *The God Delusion* (2006), Dawkins has adopted a more coherent position, arguing that the tendency of humans to behave in a universally cooperative and altruistic way is indeed quite natural, and should be seen as a 'blessed misfiring' of a mechanism which evolved initially to benefit only close relatives.

The flurry of discussion precipitated by *The Selfish Gene* partially obscured the fact that there has been a long, alternative Darwinian tradition of writers appealing to nature as teacher of sympathy, altruism, and mutual aid, rather than of struggle and self-assertion. Although Darwin's own work is more often remembered for the vivid picture it painted of struggle and conflict in nature, *The Descent of Man* (1871) also emphasized the more collaborative aspects of animal life, documenting self-sacrificing and cooperative behaviour among insects, birds, and apes, culminating in that pinnacle of evolved morality – the human conscience. Since Darwin's day, many more examples have been added, including detailed studies of the complex systems of altruism and cooperation that operate among social insects, as well as the posting of altruistic sentinels by some species of bird and mammal, who risk their own lives to warn the rest of the group of imminent danger.

So, the secular humanist can argue, we do not need to be religious, nor to believe in an afterlife, in order to be good; we simply need to follow nature. Believers may warn us that accepting a scientific view of human nature will mean that we behave like animals. But since behaving like animals, in certain cases, means sacrificing yourself for the good of others or collaborating in pursuit of a shared communal goal, then perhaps we should all behave like animals more often.

Dealing with deviance

The moral and legal codes of the monotheistic traditions reveal preoccupations with all sorts of different social problems, including how to get on with neighbouring tribes, how to deal with religious dissent, how to enforce regulations relating to many details of everyday life including diet, dress, and domestic arrangements, and how to punish those who break the rules. A theme that recurs frequently among these other subjects is sex. Sexual desire has produced as much conflict and anxiety as it has pleasure for as long as human civilizations have existed. And religions have tried to provide rules and regulations to cope with this very powerful human drive. Generally speaking, sex between men and women, within marriage, to produce children, has been approved of (although St Paul thought it was better to remain celibate), while virtually any other kind of sex, most notably sex with oneself, or with someone of the same sex, or with someone in one's own family, has normally been condemned (and sometimes considered punishable by death).

In modern societies where science and medicine have gradually taken over from traditional religious beliefs as the most acceptable sources of publicly agreed divisions between the normal and the deviant, two parallel trends can be discerned: a de-moralization of previously moral issues, but also a concomitant medical and scientific reinforcement and naturalization of existing social divisions and inequalities. Modern science has proved just as ideologically malleable as the Bible when it comes to arguing either for or against such divisions. Two examples relating to sexual ethics will offer a brief illustration of these trends.

The late 19th century saw the emergence of new ideas about homosexuality (and the very coining of the term 'homosexual'). One prevailing view until that time had been that sex between two men was an unnatural and sinful act which revealed a moral failing or a perversion of character – and one which could be identified with the suitably biblical name of 'sodomy', named after the sinful people of the towns of Sodom and Gomorrah described in the Book of Genesis. Sex between two men was not only a sin but also a crime (one that was punishable by death in Britain until 1861). The sensational conviction of Oscar Wilde for acts of gross indecency in 1895, and his sentencing to two years in prison with hard labour, drew a great deal of public attention to the question, and gradually what we might consider a more liberal and scientific approach to the question started to gain a hearing. A key figure in this movement was the sexologist Havelock Ellis, who used psychological studies of homosexual men to argue that homosexuality was natural. We should not, he argued, imprison people for acting on a natural instinct. Many decades later, in 1967, this view finally came to prevail and sex between two consenting adult men was decriminalized in Britain.

A very similar pattern can be discerned in the case of masturbation. Again, this was a practice known by a biblically inspired name – onanism. The name in this case was an allusion to the sin of Onan, who, according to the Book of Genesis, 'spilled his semen on the ground' rather than impregnating his brother's wife, as he had been told to do by his father. Genesis records that what Onan did was 'wicked in the Lord's sight; so he put him to death'. In the 18th and 19th centuries, this religious condemnation transmuted into a medical diagnosis. A widely distributed treatise entitled *Onania* denounced the 'heinous sin of self-pollution' (also known as 'self-abuse') and 'all its frightful consequences (in both sexes)'. This work combined sexual titillation with moralism and medical advice. More respectable versions of this kind of writing were produced throughout the 19th century, when it became an article of medical orthodoxy that masturbation was both a symptom and a cause of insanity and of physical debility. Unpleasant medical remedies and ingeniously punitive mechanical devices were devised to counteract this physical and moral evil. As with homosexuality, medical ideas and practices seemed to have taken over from religious and moral ones as ways of dealing with sexual deviance. The same pattern was also repeated in the context of debates about the differences between men and women, and the relationship between white colonizers and the indigenous peoples they displaced. Scientific theories about sex and race were on hand to provide new

ONANIA:

OR, THE

HEINOUS SIN

OF

𝔖𝔢𝔩𝔣=𝔓𝔬𝔩𝔩𝔲𝔱𝔦𝔬𝔫,

AND ALL ITS

FRIGHTFUL CONSEQUENCES (in Both Sexes)

CONSIDERED:

With Spiritual and Physical ADVICE to those who have already injured themselves by this abominable Practice.

The EIGHTEENTH EDITION, as also the NINTH EDITION of the *SUPPLEMENT* to it, both of them Revised and Enlarged, and now Printed together in One Volume.

As the several Passages in the *Former* Impressions, that have been charged with being obscure and ambiguous, are, in these, cleared up and explained, there will be no more Alterations or Additions made.

And ONAN knew that the Seed should not be his: And it came to pass, when he went in unto his Brother's Wife, that he spilled it on the Ground, lest that he should give Seed to his Brother. And the Thing which he did, displeased the LORD; wherefore he slew him also. Gen. xxxviii. 9, 10.

Non Quis, Sed Quid.

LONDON:

Printed for H. COOKE, at the R____ ____ Fleet-street, 1756.

[Price Bound ____ Shillings and Sixpence]

---

19. A mid-18th-century edition of the anonymous pamphlet *Onania*, first distributed in London in 1716

rationalizations of inequalities previously justified in religious and political terms.

The naturalistic fallacy

Science and religion have both been used in pursuit of all sorts of different political goals. Neither is inherently liberal or conservative, racist or egalitarian, repressive or permissive. Each provides a way of understanding the world which might be made consilient with almost any ideological vision. But while we are used to the idea that religious believers will look at ethical and political questions through the lenses of their particular faith commitments, we have not yet learned to be quite so attentive in the case of those who claim to speak for science. On the face of it, a scientific approach to ethics promises to be a balanced and objective one – and one which takes its lead from nature rather than from human prejudices. Does nature not speak with a clear and impartial voice?

Some philosophers, driven by the desire to develop a more scientific approach to morality, have constructed whole systems of 'evolutionary ethics'. For such thinkers, the fact that humanity's conscience and moral feelings are the product of evolution requires that ethics should be pursued from an evolutionary rather than a religious or even a philosophical point of view. The problem that all such schemes encounter is that there is more to ethics than following nature. Even if it can be shown that we are endowed with a particular 'natural' instinct by our evolutionary history, that observation does not get us any closer to answering the ethical question of whether it is right to follow that instinct. Presumably the instincts that incline people towards violence, theft, and adultery have evolutionary origins too. Whichever interpretation of evolutionary biology we care to endorse, it is perfectly clear (as it has been to moral philosophers through the ages) that human beings are born with the propensity both to seek their own good and also the good of (at least some) others.

The question of whether the altruistic instinct, for instance, is a natural one is completely separate from the question of whether it is one that we should follow, and to what extent. That question will be answered only by thinking about the rules and goals according to which we, individually and communally, wish to live our lives.

The mistake of supposing that something is ethically desirable just because it can be shown to be natural, or evolved, is sometimes referred to as the 'naturalistic fallacy'. This strange phrase is taken from the English philosopher G. E. Moore's 1903 book *Principia Ethica*. Here Moore stated that any system of ethics which tried, misguidedly he thought, to define the ethical predicate 'good' in terms of a naturalistic predicate such as 'pleasurable' or 'useful' or 'for the good of the species' was guilty of committing the 'naturalistic fallacy'.

Some religious thinkers have invoked the 'naturalistic fallacy' as a reason to resist all secular and scientific approaches to ethics. However, it should be pointed out that Moore's ban on translating the word 'good' into any non-ethical term was applied by him to metaphysical and philosophical systems of ethics too. In fact, Moore's view really amounted to complete moral mysticism. A system of ethics which identifies 'good' with 'in accordance with God's will' or 'for the greatest good of the greatest number', or anything else at all (apart from Moore's own favoured sense of goodness as an intuited quality of beauty) is equally guilty of committing the 'naturalistic fallacy'. From this point of view, religious and scientific approaches to ethics are each in an equally bad position.

Beyond nature

The cases of altruism and sexuality considered in this chapter both give us some sense of why we should be suspicious of any ethical or political argument that is based on what is natural. We can be drawn into these kinds of arguments from all sorts of laudable motives. For instance, campaigners against anti-homosexual laws will often cite evidence of homosexual behaviour among various species of birds and mammals in support of the view that homosexuality is natural. Modern medical orthodoxy now holds that masturbation should be not only allowed, but positively encouraged, because it is natural. Religious critics of interpretations of evolutionary biology that suggest we must resign ourselves to a society ruled by selfishness have been led to insist that, on the contrary, human altruism is not only desirable but natural. But 'natural' in these contexts really means fixed, given, determined. It denotes not the act of a free individual, but the playing out of an unalterable physical law. Political questions about what sexual behaviour should be allowed, or how the interests of different groups within society are to be balanced and regulated, are decided by human laws, not by laws of nature.

Think again about the case of homosexuality. We might take the change of the law in Britain in the 1960s as evidence of how a scientific approach to a question could replace old-fashioned religious bigotry with a more enlightened and rational policy. However, that would be to overlook several other aspects of what we might call the modern medicalization of morals. To take homosexuality out of the moral and criminal realms and place it in the realm of medicine was in several ways a repressive as much as a liberating transition. Homosexual sex was now to be considered an activity that was the preserve of a particular aberrant type of person rather than simply as something that might be indulged in by anyone. In this sense, the medical view strengthened the division between normality and deviance. Secondly, the medical model was a more strictly deterministic one. Sexuality was to be considered something unalterably given by one's biological nature rather than as an expression of individuality. Finally, this new conceptualization of homosexuality categorized it as a medical disorder. It was a natural condition towards which people should show sympathy rather than condemnation, but a disorder nonetheless. This idea was still prevalent in Britain in the 1960s when the law was changed. The continuity between religious and medical attempts to define and enforce distinctions between normality and deviance is also indicated by the fact that the few organizations today that still support the idea that homosexuality is a disease from which people need to be cured are religious groups.

In the case of altruism, religious responses to evolutionary ideas about competition and 'selfish genes' have given an exaggerated sense of the value of self-sacrifice. Recent debates about science and ethics have often proceeded as if moral goodness and altruism were synonymous. Some claim that altruism is natural and so we should follow nature. Others insist that we have evolved to be essentially selfish and so we need to struggle against nature. But both views are based on a very limited understanding of what it is to live a good life. Individualism and self-development have traditionally been valued by both secular and religious moralists. As several commentators have pointed out, when Jesus told the rich young man to sell all his possessions and give the proceeds to the poor so that he might have 'treasure in heaven', that advice was given for the good of the young man, not for the good of the poor. There are political connotations too. The ideology of altruism is one that is open to manipulation by ruling elites. The idea of living for others sounds like a noble one. But it can be used both by totalitarian governments seeking to persuade their subjects that the interests of the whole must come before their own individual rights, and also by those politicians whose objectives can only be achieved through thousands of military personnel being prepared to give up their lives in pursuit of them. I suppose that suicide bombers too might see their acts as heroically altruistic. Again, the value of altruism is something to be decided by political and moral discussion, not by an appeal to nature.

As I have already pointed out, religious ethics is in just as bad (and therefore just as good) a position as scientific ethics when it comes to justifying its attempts to derive moral guidance from facts about nature, society, humanity, or authoritative texts. Religion and science both provide resources with which people can try to make sense of the situation they find themselves in. From within a particular world view or ideology, certain maxims will seem fundamental and unalterable: for a Muslim, the truth of the Quran; for a Christian, the fact of the resurrection; for an atheist, the purely human nature of all moral codes. Neither science nor religion can determine, for some mythical neutral observer, which foundational maxims we should adopt. But they can provide concepts, beliefs, practices, rituals, and stories that can be used to piece together moral meanings.

In the modern world, it seems as though science, technology, and medicine are increasingly dominating the attempts to make such moral meanings. Instead of being warned by the great religious prophets of the past that we must mend our wicked ways or face the wrath of God and cosmic cataclysms, we are now warned that our sexual immorality, gluttony, and greed will lead to venereal disease, obesity, and the flooding, burning, and destruction of our planet as a result of catastrophic levels of global warming. The details have changed, but the essential structure is the same. Science and medicine provide us with frightening new visions of the future which policy-makers and political leaders use to try to persuade us, as did the prophets of old, to repent and change our ways before it is too late.

Looking to that future, there is every reason to believe that science and religion will both continue to flourish, to enlighten, to inspire; as well as to frustrate, to obfuscate, and to oppress.

Some people may wish that one half of this essentially modern pairing could be disposed of, or could be persuaded to relinquish its troublesome claims to authority in some or other sphere of knowledge, morality, or politics. But such people should be careful what they wish for. Would they really prefer to live in a society where everyone agreed about the questions that this book has been about? What sort of place would that be?

References and further reading

Abbreviations for websites cited more than once:

CCEL	Christian Classics Ethereal Library: http://www.ccel.org/
CWCD	The Complete Works of Charles Darwin Online: http://darwin-online.org.uk/
DCP	The Darwin Correspondence Project: http://www.darwinproject.ac.uk/
FT	Douglas O. Linder's Famous Trials site at the University of Missouri-Kansas City School of Law: http://www.umkc.edu/famoustrials/
HF	The Huxley File at Clark University: http://aleph0.clarku.edu/huxley/
NP	The Newton Project at Sussex University: http://www.newtonproject.sussex.ac.uk/
PG	Project Gutenberg: http://www.gutenberg.org/
RJLR	Rutgers Journal of Law and Religion: http://org.law.rutgers.edu/publications/law-religion/
TP	Thomas Paine National Historical Association: http://www.thomaspaine.org/

References

This section gives references for material directly quoted in the text above. The further reading section below gives suggested background reading and additional sources.

Where reputable online editions of works are available, these have been cited in addition to the original published source. Different English translations of biblical passages can be compared online at The Bible Gateway: http://www.biblegateway.com/

Chapter 1

Galileo's condemnation: Mario Biagioli, *Galileo, Courtier: The Practice of Science in the Culture of Absolutism* (Chicago, 1994), quotation at pp. 330–1. Documents relating to Galileo's trial and condemnation can be found online at FT. ♦ Psalm 102:25. ♦ Thomas Huxley's review of *On the Origin of Species* was originally published in 1860 in the *Westminster Review* and was reprinted in Volume 2 of his *Collected Essays* (9 volumes, London, 1893–4), pp. 22–79, quotation at p. 52; available online at HF. ♦ John Hedley Brooke, *Science and Religion: Some Historical Perspectives* (Cambridge, 1991), quotation at p. 5. ♦ Quotation from Galileo Galilei, *Dialogue Concerning the Two Chief World Systems* (1632), in William Shea, 'Galileo's Copernicanism: The Science and the Rhetoric', in *The Cambridge Companion to Galileo*, ed. Peter Machamer (Cambridge, 1998), pp. 211–43, quotation at p. 238. ♦ Psalm 19:1. ♦ Thomas Paine, *The Age of Reason, Part I* (1794), in *Thomas Paine: Political Writings*, ed. Bruce Kuklick (Cambridge, 1989), quotations from Chapters 7, 11, and 16; available online at TP. ♦ Altruism research: Stephen Post and Jill Neimark, *Why Good Things Happen to Good People: The Exciting New Research that Proves the Link between Doing Good and Living a Longer, Healthier, Happier Life* (New York, 2007). ♦ The medieval Islamic motto is quoted in Emilie Savage-Smith, 'The Universality and Neutrality of Science', in *Universality in Islamic Thought*, ed. Leonard Binder (forthcoming).

Chapter 2

Documents relating to Galileo's trial and condemnation can be found at FT. ♦ Francis Bacon, *The New Organon, or True Directions Concerning the Interpretation of Nature* (1620), Aphorism III; *Valerius Terminus: Of the Interpretation of Nature* (1603), Chapter 1. Both these works are available in modern editions, and also online at the University of Adelaide: http://etext.library.adelaide.edu.au/ ♦ Thomas Paine, *The Age of Reason, Part I* (1794), in *Thomas Paine: Political Writings*, ed. Bruce Kuklick (Cambridge, 1989), Chapter 2; available online at TP. ♦ Joshua 10:12–14. ♦ Council of Trent declaration: Richard Blackwell, 'Could There Be Another Galileo Case?', in *The Cambridge Companion to Galileo*, ed. Peter Machamer (Cambridge, 1998), pp. 348–66, quotation at p. 353. ♦ Romans 1:20.

Chapter 3

Milk miracle: 'Right-Wing Hindus Milk India's "Miracle"', *The Independent* (London), 25 September 1995, p. 11. ♦ Friedrich Schleiermacher, *On Religion: Speeches to its Cultured Despisers*, ed. Richard Crouter (Cambridge, 1996), Second Speech, quotation at p. 49; first published in German in 1799; available online at CCEL. ♦ Henry Drummond, *The Lowell Lectures on the Ascent of Man* (1894), Chapter 10; available online at CCEL. ♦ G. W. Leibniz, 'Mr Leibnitz's First Paper' in Samuel Clarke, *A Collection of Papers, Which passed between the late Learned Mr. Leibnitz, and Dr. Clarke, In the Years 1715 and 1716* (1717); available online at NP. ♦ Laplace and Napoleon: Roger Hahn, 'Laplace and the Mechanistic Universe', in *God and Nature: Historical Essays on the Encounter between Christianity and Science*, ed. David C. Lindberg and Ronald L. Numbers (Berkeley, 1986), pp. 256–76, quotation at p. 256. ♦ Descartes to Mersenne: quoted in Carolyn Merchant, *The Death of Nature: Women, Ecology, and the Scientific Revolution* (San Francisco, 1983), p. 205. ♦ Nancy Cartwright uses the phrase 'dappled world' to echo Gerard Manley Hopkins' poem 'Pied Beauty', which starts with the line, 'Glory be to God for dappled things'; Nancy Cartwright, *The Dappled World:*

A Study of the Boundaries of Science (Cambridge, 1999), Part I, quotation from Hopkins at p. 19. ◆ Einstein made comments about God not playing dice on several occasions, including in a letter to the physicist Max Born in 1926; Abraham Pais, *Subtle is the Lord: The Science and the Life of Albert Einstein*, new edition (Oxford, 2005), Chapter 25. ◆ Fred Hoyle, 'The Universe: Past and Present Reflections', *Engineering and Science* (November 1981), pp. 8–12; quoted in Rodney D. Holder, *God, the Multiverse, and Everything: Modern Cosmology and the Argument from Design* (Aldershot, 2004), p. 34. ◆ David Hume, *Dialogues Concerning Natural Religion* (1779), Part II; available in several modern editions, and online at PG. ◆ John 20:24–30. ◆ Thomas Paine, *The Age of Reason, Part I* (1794), in *Thomas Paine: Political Writings*, ed. Bruce Kuklick (Cambridge, 1989), Chapter 3; available online at TP. ◆ Richard Dawkins, *The Selfish Gene*, new edition (Oxford, 1989), p. 330. ◆ Fyodor Dostoyevsky, *The Brothers Karamazov*, translated with an introduction by David Magarshack (London, 1982), Book 5, Chapter 4, 'Rebellion', pp. 276–88; first published in Russian in 1880; available online at CCEL.

Chapter 4

Charles Lyell used the phrase 'go the whole orang' in a letter to Darwin in March 1863. Frederick Burkhardt and Sydney Smith (eds), *The Correspondence of Charles Darwin, Volume 11: 1863* (Cambridge, 1985), pp. 230–3; this letter is available online at DCP. ◆ Quotations from Darwin's *Beagle* notebooks: Adrian Desmond and James Moore, *Darwin* (London, 1991), pp. 122, 176. ◆ Darwin's comments on the 'damnable doctrine' of damnation, and on preferring the label 'Agnostic', are made in the section of his autobiography concerning religious belief, *The Autobiography of Charles Darwin*, ed. Nora Barlow (London, 1958), pp. 85–96, quotations at pp. 87, 94; available online at CWCD. ◆ Darwin's exclamation 'What a book a Devil's chaplain might write' was in a letter to Joseph Hooker in July 1856, Frederick Burkhardt and Sydney Smith (eds), *The Correspondence of Charles Darwin, Volume 6: 1856–1857* (Cambridge, 1985), pp. 178–80; this letter is available online at DCP. ♦ The letter about the afterlife from Emma to Charles, and his additional note on it, are quoted in Adrian Desmond and James Moore, *Darwin* (London, 1991), pp. 280–1, 651. ♦ Darwin's comments about Lyell's impact on his view of the natural world were made in a letter to Leonard Horner in August 1844, Frederick Burkhardt and Sydney Smith (eds), *The Correspondence of Charles Darwin, Volume 3: 1844–1846* (Cambridge, 1985), pp. 54–5; this letter is available online at DCP. ♦ Tortoise soup: Charles Darwin, 'Galapagos. Otaheite Lima', *Beagle* field notebook EH1.17, 12 October 1835, p. 36b; available online at CWCD. ♦ *On the Origin of Species by Means of Natural Selection* (1859) is available in many modern editions, and online at CWCD, where changes between editions can also be compared, such as the insertion of 'by the Creator' at the end of the 1860 second edition, at p. 490. ♦ Charles Kingsley, *The Water Babies* (1863), Chapter 7, p. 315; available online at PG. ♦ Samuel Wilberforce's review of *On the Origin of Species* first appeared in the *Quarterly Review* 108 (1860), pp. 225–64, quotations at pp. 231, 259–60; available online at CWCD. ♦ Huxley's and others' recollections of the 1860 Oxford debate are discussed in Frank James, 'An "Open Clash between Science and the Church"? Wilberforce, Huxley and Hooker on Darwin at the British Association, Oxford, 1860', in *Science and Beliefs: From Natural Philosophy to Natural Science, 1700–1900*, ed. D. Knight and M. Eddy (Aldershot, 2005), pp. 171–93, quotation from Huxley at p. 185. See also Leonard Huxley, *The Life and Letters of Thomas Henry Huxley*, 2 vols (London, 1900); selections available online through the '20th Century Commentary' section of HF. ♦ The text of Pope Benedict XVI's homily on the occasion of his inaugural Mass on Sunday, 24 April 2005 is available in the online 'Papal Archive' at 'Vatican: The Holy See': http://www.vatican.va/

Chapter 5

The American Association for the Advancement of Science statement on 'Intelligent Design' was approved by its Board of Directors in October 2002. The text is available online through their website via an archived news release dated 6 November 2002; a related AAAS news release and statement on 'Anti-Evolution Laws' is dated 19 February 2006: http://www.aaas.org/news/ ♦ The full text of Judge John E. Jones III's ruling in the Dover case in 2005 is available on the website of the US District Court for the Middle District of Pennsylvania: http://www.pamd.uscourts.gov/kitzmiller/kitzmiller_342.pdf ♦ George Coyne's comments: 'Intelligent Design belittles God, Vatican director says' by Mark Lombard, *Catholic Online*, 30 January 2006; http://www.catholic.org/ ♦ Tennessee's 1925 anti-evolution statute is quoted in Edward J. Larson, *Summer for the Gods: The Scopes Trial and America's Continuing Debate over Science and Religion* (Cambridge, MA, 1997), p. 50. The text of the statute is available online at FT. ♦ Bryan's comments on 'the little circle entitled "Mammals"' come from the speech he intended to deliver to the jury as the closing argument for the prosecution in the Scopes trial. Darrow's decision to submit the case to the jury without argument prevented Bryan from delivering the speech, which is included as an Appendix to William Jennings Bryan and Mary Baird Bryan, *The Memoirs of William Jennings Bryan* (Philadelphia, 1925), quotation at p. 535. ♦ Genesis 1:26. ♦ Extracts from the transcript of the Scopes trial, including the cross-examination of Bryan by Darrow, are available online at FT. ♦ Thomas Jefferson's famous words, 'a wall of separation between Church and state', were used by him in a letter of 1 January 1802 to the Danbury Baptist Association. The text of the letter and an article about its restoration are available online at the Library of Congress website: http://www.loc.gov/loc/lcib/9806/danbury.html ♦ US Supreme Court opinions on *Epperson v. Arkansas* (1968) and *Edwards v. Aguillard* (1987) are available online at Cornell University Law School's 'Supreme Court Collection': http://www.law.cornell.edu/supct/index.html ♦ Bryan's comments on school board elections were made in a statement entitled 'Who shall control?', written in 1925 and included as an Appendix to William Jennings Bryan and Mary Baird Bryan, *The Memoirs of William Jennings Bryan* (Philadelphia, 1925), pp. 526–8. ♦ District Judge William R. Overton's ruling in *McLean v. Arkansas* (1982) is included as an Appendix to Langdon Gilkey, *Creationism on Trial: Evolution and God at Little Rock*

(Charlottesville, 1998), quotation at p. 295. Overton's judgment is available online at 'TalkOrigins Archive. Exploring the Creation/ Evolution Controversy': http://www.talkorigins.org/faqs/mclean-v-arkansas.html ♦ Percival W. Davis, Dean H. Kenyon, and Charles B. Thaxton, *Of Pandas and People: The Central Question of Biological Origins*, 2nd edition (Dallas, 1993).

Chapter 6

On Persinger's 'God helmet': David Biello, 'Searching for God in the Brain', *Scientific American Mind*, October 2007; available online at: http://www.sciam.com/ ♦ Mario Beauregard and Vincent Paquette, 'Neural Correlates of a Mystical Experience in Carmelite Nuns', *Neuroscience Letters*, vol. 405, issue 3, 25 September 2006, pp. 186–90; reported in *The Daily Telegraph* (London), 30 August 2006, p. 12, as 'Nuns Prove God Is Not Figment of the Mind'; available online via http://www.telegraph.co.uk/ ♦ Genesis 3:19; Ecclesiastes 3:19–20; 1 Corinthians 15. ♦ On the creeds: Peter van Inwagen, 'Dualism and Materialism: Athens and Jerusalem?', in *Christian Philosophy and the Mind-Body Problem: Faith and Philosophy*, ed. W. Hasker, vol. 12, no. 4 (1995), pp. 475–88, quotations at p. 478. ♦ George Eliot, *Middlemarch*, edited with an introduction and notes by Rosemary Ashton (London, 1994), p. 838; originally published in 1871–2; available online at the University of Virginia Library's 'Electronic Text Center': http://etext.lib.virginia.edu/ebooks/ ♦ Eric Lax, *Woody Allen: A Biography* (New York, 1992), p. 183. ♦ Isaac Watts, *Divine and Moral Songs for Children* (New York, 1866), pp. 47–8; first published as *Divine Songs* (1715); available online at CCEL. ♦ 'Let us eat and drink for tomorrow we die' is a biblical phrase: 1 Corinthians 15:32; see also Ecclesiastes 8:15, Isaiah 22:13, Luke 12:19–20. ♦ Francis Collins on altruism: *The Language of God: A Scientist Presents Evidence for Belief* (New York, 2006), pp. 21–31. ♦ Richard Dawkins on altruism: *The Selfish Gene*, new edition (Oxford, 1989), quotations at pp. 3, 200–1; *The God Delusion* (London, 2006), pp. 214–22. ♦ Sodom and Gomorrah: Genesis 18:16–19:29. ♦ Onan: Genesis 38:1–10. ♦ Rich young man: Mark 10:17–31.

Further reading

General

Reference works

Philip Clayton and Zachary Simpson (eds), *The Oxford Handbook of Religion and Science* (Oxford and New York, 2006).

Gary B. Ferngren (ed.), *The History of Science and Religion in the Western Tradition: An Encyclopedia* (New York and London, 2000).

J. Wentzel van Huyssteen (ed.), *Encyclopedia of Science and Religion*, 2 vols (New York, 2003).

Historical studies

John Hedley Brooke, *Science and Religion: Some Historical Perspectives* (Cambridge, 1991).

John Brooke and Geoffrey Cantor, *Reconstructing Nature: The Engagement of Science and Religion* (Edinburgh, 1998).

Gary B. Ferngren (ed.), *Science and Religion: A Historical Introduction* (Baltimore, 2002).

Peter Harrison, *The Bible, Protestantism, and the Rise of Natural Science* (Cambridge, 1998).

David Knight and Matthew Eddy (eds), *Science and Beliefs: From Natural Philosophy to Natural Science* (Aldershot, 2005).

David C. Lindberg and Ronald L. Numbers (eds), *God and Nature: Historical Essays on the Encounter between Christianity and Science* (Berkeley, 1986), and *When Science and Christianity Meet* (Chicago and London, 2003).

Don O'Leary, *Roman Catholicism and Modern Science: A History* (New York, 2006).

Overviews from Christian perspectives

Ian Barbour, *Religion and Science: Historical and Contemporary Issues* (San Francisco, 1997).

Alister E. McGrath, *Science and Religion: An Introduction* (Oxford, 1998).

Arthur Peacocke, *Creation and the World of Science: The Reshaping of Belief*, revised edition (Oxford and New York, 2004).

John Polkinghorne, *Theology and Science: An Introduction* (London, 1998).

Islam and Islamic science

Karen Armstrong, *Islam: A Short History* (London, 2001).

Michael Cook, *The Koran: A Very Short Introduction* (Oxford, 2000).

Muzaffar Iqbal, *Islam and Science* (Aldershot, 2002), and *Science and Islam* (Westport, 2007).

Seyyed Hossein Nasr, *Science and Civilisation in Islam*, 2nd edition (Cambridge, 1987).

Malise Ruthven, *Islam: A Very Short Introduction* (Oxford, 1997).

George Saliba, *Islamic Science and the Making of the European Renaissance* (Cambridge, MA, 2007).

Judaism and science

Geoffrey Cantor, *Quakers, Jews, and Science: Religious Responses to Modernity and the Sciences in Britain, 1650–1900* (Oxford and New York, 2005).

Geoffrey Cantor and Marc Swelitz (eds), *Jewish Tradition and the Challenge of Darwinism* (Chicago, 2006).

Noah J. Efron, *Judaism and Science: A Historical Introduction* (Westport, 2007).

International perspectives

Fraser Watts and Kevin Dutton (eds), *Why the Science and Religion Dialogue Matters: Voices from the International Society for Science and Religion* (Philadelphia and London, 2006).

Websites

American Assocation for the Advancement of Science: http://www.aaas.org/

Center for Islam and Science: http://www.cis-ca.org/

Center for Theology and the Natural Sciences: http://www.ctns.org/

International Society for Science and Religion: http://www.issr.org.uk/

John Templeton Foundation: http://www.templeton.org/

Metanexus Institute on Religion, Science, and the Humanities: http://www.metanexus.net/

National Center for Science Education: http://www.natcenscied.org/

Stanford Encyclopedia of Philosophy: http://plato.stanford.edu/

TalkOrigins Archive: Exploring the Evolution/Creation Controversy: http://www.talkorigins.org/

Chapter 1

Religious belief and the birth of modern science

Peter Dear, *Revolutionizing the Sciences: European Knowledge and its Ambitions, 1500–1700* (Basingstoke, 2001).

Rob Iliffe, *Newton: A Very Short Introduction* (Oxford, 2007).

Steven Shapin, *The Scientific Revolution* (Chicago, 1996).

Books by religious scientists

Francis Collins, *The Language of God: A Scientist Presents Evidence for Belief* (New York, 2006).

Guy Consolmagno, *God's Mechanics: How Scientists and Engineers Make Sense of Religion* (San Francisco, 2007).

Owen Gingerich, *God's Universe* (Cambridge, MA, 2006).

John Polkinghorne, *Belief in God in an Age of Science* (New Haven, 1998).

Thomas Paine

Thomas Paine, *Political Writings*, ed. Bruce Kuklick (Cambridge, 1989); Paine's major works are available online at TP.

Gregory Claeys, *Thomas Paine: Social and Political Thought* (Boston and London, 1989).

John Keane, *Tom Paine: A Political Life* (London, 1996).

Science and atheism

Richard Dawkins, *The Blind Watchmaker*, revised edition (London, 1991), and *The God Delusion* (London, 2006).

Christopher Hitchens, *God is Not Great: The Case Against Religion* (London, 2007).

Victor J. Stenger, *God: The Failed Hypothesis. How Science Shows that God Does Not Exist* (Amherst, 2007).

Natural theology

John Brooke and Geoffrey Cantor, *Reconstructing Nature: The Engagement of Science and Religion* (Edinburgh, 1998).

William Paley, *Natural Theology, or Evidence of the Existence and Attributes of the Deity, Collected from the Appearances of Nature*, edited with an introduction and notes by Matthew D. Eddy and David Knight (Oxford and New York, 2006); first published 1802.

Chapter 2

Philosophy of science

A. F. Chalmers, *What Is This Thing Called Science?*, 3rd edition (Buckingham, 1999).

Peter Godfrey-Smith, *Theory and Reality: An Introduction to the Philosophy of Science* (Chicago, 2003).

Samir Okasha, *Philosophy of Science: A Very Short Introduction* (Oxford, 2002).

Philosophy of science in theological perspective

Philip Clayton, *Explanation from Physics to Theology: An Essay in Rationality and Religion* (New Haven, 1989).

Christopher Knight, *Wrestling with the Divine: Religion, Science, and Revelation* (Minneapolis, 2001).

Galileo and the Church

John Brooke and Geoffrey Cantor, *Reconstructing Nature: The Engagement of Science and Religion* (Edinburgh, 1998), Chapter 4.

David C. Lindberg, 'Galileo, the Church, and the Cosmos', in *When Science and Christianity Meet*, ed. David C. Lindberg and Ronald L. Numbers (Chicago and London, 2003), pp. 33–60.

Peter Machamer (ed.), *The Cambridge Companion to Galileo* (Cambridge, 1998).

Stephen Mason, 'Galileo's Scientific Discoveries, Cosmological Confrontations, and the Aftermath', *History of Science*, 40 (2002), pp. 377–406.

Ernan McMullin (ed.), *The Church and Galileo* (Notre Dame, 2005).

Realism, philosophy, and science

Ian Hacking, *Representing and Intervening* (Cambridge, 1983).

Thomas Kuhn, *The Structure of Scientific Revolutions*, 3rd edition (Chicago and London, 1996); first published 1962.

Peter Lipton, *Inference to the Best Explanation*, 2nd edition (London, 2004).

Richard Rorty, *Philosophy and Social Hope* (London, 1999).

Bas van Fraassen, *The Scientific Image* (Oxford, 1980).

Realism and theology

Colin Crowder (ed.), *God and Reality: Essays on Christian Non-Realism* (London, 1997).

Don Cupitt, *Taking Leave of God* (London, 1980).

Michael Scott and Andrew Moore (eds), *Realism and Religion: Philosophical and Theological Perspectives* (Aldershot, 2007).

Janet Soskice, *Metaphor and Religious Language* (Oxford, 1985).

Chapter 3

Lourdes

Ruth Harris, *Lourdes: Body and Spirit in the Secular Age* (London, 1999).

Philosophy of miracles

David Corner, *The Philosophy of Miracles* (London, 2007).

Mark Corner, *Signs of God: Miracles and Their Interpretation* (Aldershot, 2005).

History of attitudes to miracles

Robert B. Mullin, *Miracles and the Modern Religious Imagination* (New Haven and London, 1996).

Jane Shaw, *Miracles in Enlightenment England* (New Haven and London, 2006).

Hume on miracles

John Earman, *Hume's Abject Failure: The Argument Against Miracles* (New York, 2000).

Robert J. Fogelin, *A Defense of Hume on Miracles* (Princeton, 2003).

God and physics

Philip Clayton, *God and Contemporary Science* (Edinburgh, 1997).

Paul Davies, *The Mind of God: Science and the Search for Ultimate Meaning* (London, 1992).

Willem B. Drees, *Beyond the Big Bang: Quantum Cosmologies and God* (La Salle, 1990).

John Polkinghorne, *The Faith of a Physicist* (Princeton, 1994), also published as *Science and Christian Belief* (London, 1994).

Nicholas Saunders, *Divine Action and Modern Science* (Cambridge, 2002).

Laws of nature

Nancy Cartwright, *How the Laws of Physics Lie* (Oxford, 1983), and *The Dappled World: A Study of the Boundaries of Science* (Cambridge, 1999).

John Dupré, *The Disorder of Things: Metaphysical Foundations of the Disunity of Science* (Cambridge, MA, 1993).

Bas van Fraassen, *Laws and Symmetry* (Oxford, 1989).

Quantum physics

George Johnson, *Fire in the Mind: Science, Faith, and the Search for Order* (New York, 1995), Chapters 5 and 6.

John Polkinghorne, *Quantum Theory: A Very Short Introduction* (Oxford, 2002), and *Quantum Physics and Theology: An Unexpected Kinship* (London, 2007).

Cosmic fine tuning

Paul Davies, *The Goldilocks Enigma: Why is the Universe Just Right for Life?* (London and New York, 2006).

Rodney D. Holder, *God, the Multiverse, and Everything: Modern Cosmology and the Argument from Design* (Aldershot, 2004).

Chapter 4

Biographies of Charles Darwin

Janet Browne, *Darwin: A Biography*, 2 vols (London, 1995, 2002).

Charles Darwin, *The Autobiography of Charles Darwin*, ed. Nora Barlow (London, 1958), available online at CWCD.

Adrian Desmond and James Moore, *Darwin* (London, 1991).

Adrian Desmond, James Moore, and Janet Browne, *Charles Darwin* (Oxford, 2007).

History of biology

Peter J. Bowler, *Evolution: The History of an Idea*, 3rd edition (Berkeley and London, 2003), and *The Eclipse of Darwinism: Anti-Darwinian Evolution Theories in the Decades around 1900*, new edition (Baltimore, 1992).

Jim Endersby, *A Guinea Pig's History of Biology: The Plants and Animals Who Taught Us the Facts of Life* (London, 2007).

Darwinism and religion

Craig Baxter, *Re: Design, An Adaptation of the Correspondence of Charles Darwin, Asa Gray and Others* (2007); a dramatization, the script of which is available online at DCP.

Peter J. Bowler, *Monkey Trials and Gorilla Sermons: Evolution and Christianity from Darwin to Intelligent Design* (Cambridge, MA and London, 2007).

John Hedley Brooke, *Science and Religion: Some Historical Perspectives* (Cambridge, 1991), Chapter 8; and 'Darwin and Victorian Christianity', in *The Cambridge Companion to Darwin*, ed. Jonathan Hodge and Gregory Radick (Cambridge, 2003), pp. 192–213.

James Moore, *The Post-Darwinian Controversies: A Study of the Protestant Struggle to Come to Terms with Darwin in Great Britain and America, 1870–1900* (Cambridge, 1979), and *The Darwin Legend* (Grand Rapids, 1994).

Michael Ruse, *Darwin and Design: Does Evolution Have a Purpose?* (Cambridge, MA, 2003).

Thomas Huxley and Victorian science

Adrian Desmond, *Huxley: From Devil's Disciple to Evolution's High Priest* (London, 1998).

Frank James, 'An "Open Clash between Science and the Church"? Wilberforce, Huxley and Hooker on Darwin at the British Association, Oxford, 1860', in *Science and Beliefs: From Natural Philosophy to Natural Science, 1700–1900*, ed. D. Knight and M. Eddy (Aldershot, 2005), pp. 171–93.

Bernard Lightman (ed.), *Victorian Science in Context* (Chicago, 1997).

Frank M. Turner, *Contesting Cultural Authority: Essays in Victorian Intellectual Life* (Cambridge, 1993).

Paul White, *Thomas Huxley: Making the 'Man of Science'* (Cambridge, 2003).

Theology and evolution

Geoffrey Cantor and Marc Swelitz (eds), *Jewish Tradition and the Challenge of Darwinism* (Chicago, 2006).

John F. Haught, *God After Darwin: A Theology of Evolution* (Boulder and Oxford, 2000).

Nancey Murphy and William R. Stoeger, SJ (eds), *Evolution and Emergence: Systems, Organisms, Persons* (Oxford, 2007).

Arthur Peacocke, *Theology for a Scientific Age: Being and Becoming – Natural, Divine, and Human*, enlarged edition (Minneapolis and London, 1993).

Michael Ruse, *Can a Darwinian Be a Christian? The Relationship between Science and Religion* (Cambridge and New York, 2001).

Pierre Teilhard de Chardin, *The Phenomenon of Man*, with an introduction by Sir Julian Huxley, revised edition (London and New York, 1975); first published in French in 1955.

Chapter 5

Overview

Eugenie C. Scott, *Evolution versus Creationism: An Introduction* (Westport, 2004).

The Scopes trial

Edward J. Larson, *Summer for the Gods: The Scopes Trial and America's Continuing Debate over Science and Religion* (New York, 1997).

Fundamentalism and creationism in America

George Marsden, *Fundamentalism and American Culture*, 2nd edition (New York and Oxford, 2006).

Dorothy Nelkin, *The Creation Controversy: Science or Scripture in the Schools?* (New York, 1982).

Ronald L. Numbers, *The Creationists: From Scientific Creationism to Intelligent Design*, expanded edition (Cambridge, MA and London, 2006).

Christopher P. Toumey, *God's Own Scientists: Creationists in a Secular World* (New Brunswick, 1994).

Legal aspects

Langdon Gilkey, *Creationism on Trial: Evolution and God at Little Rock* (Charlottesville, 1998).

Philip A. Italiano, '*Kitzmiller v. Dover Area School District*: The First Judicial Test for Intelligent Design', *Rutgers Journal of Law and Religion*, vol. 8.1, Fall 2006, available online at RJLR.

Marcel La Follette (ed.), *Creationism, Science, and the Law: The Arkansas Case* (Cambridge, MA, 1983).

Edward J. Larson, *Trial and Error: The American Controversy over Creation and Evolution*, 3rd edition (New York and Oxford, 2003).

Stephen A. Newman, 'Evolution and the Holy Ghost of Scopes: Can Science Lose the Next Round?', *Rutgers Journal of Law and Religion*, vol. 8.2, Spring 2007, available online at RJLR.

Intelligent Design and its critics

Michael J. Behe, *Darwin's Black Box: The Biochemical Challenge to Evolution* (New York, 1996), and *The Edge of Evolution: The Search for the Limits of Darwinism* (New York, 2007).

William Dembski and Michael Ruse (eds), *Debating Design: From Darwin to DNA* (Cambridge, 2004).

Kenneth R. Miller, *Finding Darwin's God: A Scientist's Search for Common Ground between God and Evolution* (New York, 1999).

Randy Olson (writer and director), *Flock of Dodos: The Evolution-Intelligent Design Circus* (Prairie Starfish Productions and G-7 Animation, documentary film, 2006).

Robert T. Pennock (ed.), *Intelligent Design Creationism and Its Critics: Philosophical, Theological, and Scientific Perspectives* (Cambridge, MA, 2001).

Philosophical perspectives

David Hull and Michael Ruse (eds), *The Philosohpy of Biology* (Oxford, 1998), Part X.

Michael Ruse (ed.), *But Is It Science? The Philosophical Question in the Creation/Evolution Controversy* (Amherst, 1996).

Sahotra Sarkar, *Doubting Darwin? Creationist Designs on Evolution* (Malden and Oxford, 2007).

Chapter 6

Brain and mind

Antonio Damasio, *Descartes' Error: Emotion, Reason, and the Human Brain*, revised edition (London, 2006).

John Searle, *Mind: A Brief Introduction* (Oxford, 2004).

Neuroscience, psychology, and religion

C. Daniel Batson, Patricia Schoenrade, and W. Larry Ventis, *Religion and the Individual: A Social-Psychological Perspective* (New York and Oxford, 1993).

Warren S. Brown, Nancey Murphy, and H. Newton Malony, *Whatever Happened to the Soul? Scientific and Theological Portraits of Human Nature* (Minneapolis, 1998).

William James, *The Varieties of Religious Experience: A Study in Human Nature*, centenary edition with introductions by Eugene Taylor and Jeremy Carrette (London and New York, 2002); first published 1902.

Andrew Newberg, Eugene d'Aquili, and Vince Rause, *Why God Won't Go Away: Brain Science and the Biology of Belief* (New York, 2002).

Fraser Watts, *Theology and Psychology* (Aldershot, 2002).

Cognitive science and anthropology of religion

Scott Atran, *In Gods We Trust: The Evolutionary Landscape of Religion* (London and New York, 2002).

Pascal Boyer, *Religion Explained: The Human Instincts that Fashion Gods, Spirits and Ancestors* (London, 2001).

Steven Mithen, *The Prehistory of the Mind: The Search for the Origins of Art, Religion and Science* (London, 1996).

Wentzel van Huyssteen, *Alone in the World? Human Uniqueness in Science and Theology: The Gifford Lectures* (Grand Rapids, 2006).

Evolution and ethics

Stephen R. L. Clark, *Biology and Christian Ethics* (Cambridge, 2000).

Daniel C. Dennett, *Darwin's Dangerous Idea: Evolution and the Meanings of Life* (London and New York, 1995).

Frans de Waal, *Primates and Philosophers: How Morality Evolved* (Princeton and Oxford, 2006).

Thomas Huxley, *Evolution and Ethics, and Other Essays*, in *Collected Essays* (London, 1893–4), vol. 9; available online at HF.

Mary Midgley, *Beast and Man: The Roots of Human Nature*, new edition (London and New York, 1995).

Matt Ridley, *The Origins of Virtue* (London, 1996).

Altruism and selfishness

Richard Dawkins, *The Selfish Gene* (New York and Oxford, 1976), also
available in a revised 1989 edition, and a 30th anniversary edition
with a new introduction by the author published in 2006.

Thomas Dixon, *The Invention of Altruism: Making Moral Meanings
in Victorian Britain* (Oxford, 2008).

Stephen G. Post, Lynn G. Underwood, Jeffrey P. Schloss, and William
B. Hurlbut (eds), *Altruism and Altruistic Love: Science, Philosophy
and Religion in Dialogue* (Oxford and New York, 2002).

Eliott Sober and David Sloan Wilson, *Unto Others: The Evolution and
Psychology of Unselfish Behavior* (Cambridge, MA and London,
1998).

Deviance and sexuality

Thomas Laqueur, *Solitary Sex: A Cultural History of Masturbation*
(New York, 2003).

Roy Porter and Lesley Hall, *The Facts of Life: The Creation of Sexual
Knowledge in Britain, 1650–1950* (New Haven, 1995).

Jeffrey Weeks, *Sex, Politics and Society: The Regulation of Sexuality
since 1800*, 2nd edition (London, 1989), and *Coming Out:
Homosexual Politics in Britain from the Nineteenth Century to the
Present*, revised edition (London, 1990).

Moore and the naturalistic fallacy

Alasdair MacIntyre, *After Virtue: A Study in Moral Theory*, 2nd
edition (Notre Dame, 1984).

G. E. Moore, *Principia Ethica*, edited with an introduction by Thomas
Baldwin (Cambridge, 1993); first published 1903.

Science and the future

Stephen R. L. Clark, *How to Live Forever: Science Fiction and
Philosophy* (London and New York, 1995).

Mary Midgley, *Science as Salvation: A Modern Myth and Its Meaning*
(London and New York, 1992), and *Evolution as a Religion:
Strange Hopes and Stranger Fears*, revised edition (London and
New York, 2002).

John Polkinghorne and Michael Welker (eds), *The End of the World
and the Ends of God: Science and Theology on Eschatology*
(Harrisburg, 2000).

Index

G

H

I

J

Index

149

U

V

W

Y

Z

GALILEO
A Very Short Introduction
Stillman Drake

Galileo's scientific method was of overwhelming significance for the development of modern physics, and led to a final parting of the ways between science and philosophy.

In a startling reinterpretation of the evidence, Stillman Drake advances the hypothesis that Galileo's trial and condemnation by the Inquisition in 1633 was caused not by his defiance of the Church, but by the hostility of contemporary philosophers.

Galileo's own beautifully lucid arguments are used to show how his scientific method was utterly divorced from the Aristotelian approach to physics in that it was based on a search not for causes but for laws.

'stimulating and very convincing'

Theology

www.oup.co.uk/isbn/0-19-285456-9

PHILOSOPHY
A Very Short Introduction
Edward Craig

This lively and engaging book is the ideal introduction for anyone who has ever been puzzled by what philosophy is or what it is for.

Edward Craig argues that philosophy is not an activity from another planet: learning about it is just a matter of broadening and deepening what most of us do already. He shows that philosophy is no mere intellectual pastime: thinkers such as Plato, Buddhist writers, Descartes, Hobbes, Hume, Hegel, Darwin, Mill and de Beauvoir were responding to real needs and events – much of their work shapes our lives today, and many of their concerns are still ours.

'A vigorous and engaging introduction that speaks to the philosopher in everyone.'

John Cottingham, University of Reading

'addresses many of the central philosophical questions in an engaging and thought-provoking style . . . Edward Craig is already famous as the editor of the best long work on philosophy (the Routledge Encyclopedia); now he deserves to become even better known as the author of one of the best short ones.'

Nigel Warburton, The Open University

www.oup.co.uk/isbn/0-19-285421-6